SO YOU WANT TO GO INTO THE THEATRE?

SO YOU WANT TO GO INTO THE THEATRE?

A "Manual"

BY

SHEPARD TRAUBE

FOREWORD BY
BARRETT H. CLARK

BOSTON
LITTLE, BROWN, AND COMPANY
1936

Copyright, 1936,

BY SHEPARD TRAUBE

———

All rights reserved

Published October, 1936

PRINTED IN THE UNITED STATES OF AMERICA

ISBN: 0-9820733-9-9
Digitally Reproduced in 2009 by:
Converpage
23 Acorn Street
Scituate, MA 02066
www.converpage.com

TO
KENNETH MACGOWAN

TO THE UNINITIATED

If you want to go into the theatre, you should be told that the odds are against you. You have one chance in a thousand — ask anyone who knows.

You have no way of proving you have talent until you've proved it.

The professional theatre is centered in New York and New York pays no attention to unknowns.

The chances are that you're wasting your time, if you make the plunge.

The intent of this book is to present the facts as they exist. Everything about this book is supposed to be discouraging.

You've probably already been warned how hard it is to become a success in the theatre. It probably has had very little effect on you, and you probably won't pay too much attention to the cold statistics which crop up in this book.

Well, you're quite right — if you have talent and nerve, the fact remains that there *is* a chance for you in the theatre and the information contained in this book may be valuable to you.

On the other hand, you may be disturbed by some of the cold facts and your fine enthusiasm dampened.

So read it at your peril!

THE AUTHOR

In this its 50th year, Stage Directors and Choreographers Society proudly shares with you and everyone "*who wants to go into the theatre*" this reprint of our Founder, Shepard Traube's 1938 book. Break a leg!

Special thanks to Vicki and Elizabeth Traube

THE 50 FOR THE 50TH HONORARY COMMITTEE CHAIR
Hal Prince

THE 50 FOR THE 50TH HONORARY COMMITTEE

JoAnne Akalaitis
Edward Albee
Pat Birch
Peter Brook
Arvin Brown
Robert Brustein
James Burrows
Wayne Cilento
Martha Clarke
Hope Clarke
Graciela Daniele
Gordon Davidson
Gemze de Lappe
Carmen de Lavallade
André De Shields
John Dillon
Sheldon Epps
Oskar Eustis
Zelda Fichandler
Michael Greif
Edward Hastings
Nagle Jackson
Michael Kahn
Terry Kinney
Michael Langham
James Lapine
Gillian Lynne
Des McAnuff
Joe Mantello
Rob Marshall
Michael Mayer
Lynne Meadow
Sam Mendes
Jerry Mitchell
Mike Nichols
Trevor Nunn
Jack O'Brien
Austin Pendleton
Hal Prince
Ann Reinking
Donald Saddler
Susan Stroman
Julie Taymor
Twyla Tharp
Tommy Tune
Paul Weidner
Stan Wojewodski, Jr.
George C. Wolfe
Jerry Zaks
Mary Zimmerman

PRESIDENT
Karen Azenberg

EXECUTIVE VICE PRESIDENT
Larry Carpenter

VICE PRESIDENT
Kathleen Marshall

TREASURER
Doug Hughes

SECRETARY
Mary Robinson

EXECUTIVE BOARD

Julie Arenal
Rob Ashford
Walter Bobbie
Joe Calarco
Tisa Chang
Edie Cowan
Marcia Milgrom Dodge
Gerald Freedman
Michael John Garcés
Wendy C. Goldberg
Richard Hamburger
Sue Lawless
Paul Lazarus
Ethan McSweeny
Tom Moore
Amy Morton
Sharon Ott
Lisa Peterson
Lonny Price
Susan H. Schulman
Oz Scott
Leigh Silverman
Daniel Sullivan
David Warren
Chay Yew

HONORARY ADVISORY COMMITTEE
Pamela Berlin
Melvin Bernhardt
Julianne Boyd
Danny Daniels
Barbara Hauptman
Marshall W. Mason
Ted Pappas
Gene Saks

Many years ago I was active on the Board of the SSDC (now SDC) and my memory has no sharper images of those early years than Mildred Traube, handing out letters, notices and documents from a sheaf of papers in her arms while hovering over the seated members of the Board, and Shepard Traube hovering over Mildred.

Fifty years ago our leadership meetings seemed more store-front than corporate, more invented than conforming, but regardless of their ad-hoc nature, Shep Traube thrived on the certainty that the Society could protect our artistic rights, promote a living wage and create a significant health and pension plan. Where Shep consistently outshined the rest of us was his utter delight in executing these tasks and the energy he supplied his "brothers" to complete them. He was our founder and first President and through his lifetime never reduced his involvement or concern for the Society.

Shep was the personification of a Broadway Stage Director credited with such stupefying hits as "Angel Street" which ran for 1,295 performances, and a few obligatory failures like "The Sophisticrats". From October 1931 to December 1975, he directed 19 plays and musicals and produced most of them under his own banner, amazing when you consider today's rosters. He had sufficient distain for Hollywood to fully qualify as a stage director and chronicled many of his West Coast observations with the novel, *Glory Road*.

It is rumored his love for the stage caused him to nurture actors, writers, designers and stagehands with more care than his children. And in return, for the more than 40 years as a Director, producer and foresighted union organizer he is venerated by the theatre world. The book you are about to read, *So You Want to go into the Theatre?* contains lots of facts, humorous anecdotes and much wisdom and as such, is a wonderful read and a lovely commemorative gift. Yet no words can adequately describe the joy which resulted in the salivation on Shep's lips as he untangled "irreconcilable" problems with the League of Broadway Producers, or the sly twinkle in his eyes when he suggested to the nascent League of Regional Theatres that the SSDC be recognized as the sole bargaining unit for all stage Directors. Those of us who knew him were lucky, and many of us are still here to talk about it; those thousands of others who came after and are shadowing his footsteps have simply had a better life in the American Theatre because of Shepard Traube.

Ed Sherin
Director, Member of SDC
November, 2009

FOREWORD

If Shepard Traube were anyone but the determined man he is I might feel pride in and claim a little credit for this book of his, because when he first came to me and told me what he wanted to do I caught some of his enthusiasm and before the end of our talk I half imagined I was actually working on what at that first visit was only the shadow of an idea. It is quite true I ventured to tell him what I would do if I had had the idea, and till the day he brought me the finished work I kept after him, adding from time to time a few notions of my own that I imagined might help. Now, ordinarily such proddings are necessary with active and energetic young men who say they are writing books, but it was not so with Shepard Traube. He was always several jumps ahead of me. "Why", I would occasionally ask him, "don't you tell about such and such? That certainly belongs." "See chapter seven", he would snap back. "Got it all there." He had.

And when he dumped the completed manuscript in front of me he modestly asked my advice, wanted suggestions, demanded to know where he was wrong. So I read the whole thing through, and the few minor details I could even argue about seemed so unimportant that I was afraid he might think I hadn't read what he had written. But I had — with admiration and deep interest, and with gratitude.

True, I couldn't claim even to have been part father to the work, because the author is the kind of man who sees through what he starts, and I could even with less justification believe I had kept him at work by encouraging him; he needed no encouragement. I seriously doubt if he needs this little prefatory note; if he did he would have put it into its proper place ("See chapter seven"!); but *I* need it, just to be able to tell anyone who wants to go into the theatre that this is not only the best book on the subject, but the only one, and so far as I can see it will keep others from trying to do the same thing. All he needs to do is to bring it up to date every once in a while.

I like this book because it answers briefly, accurately, and honestly, those questions that some thousands of young men and women who want to devote themselves to the theatre are always asking, questions that must be answered, that until this book was written no one person or agency was able to answer. Mr. Traube had no ax to grind; it meant little or nothing to him personally how many stage-struck youngsters came to New York in search of work; he is not an agent looking for business, nor an actor afraid of competition, and when he produces his next play he will know just where to go for what he needs.

Foreword

For a young man he has an honorable record on Broadway, having engaged in the production, management, and direction of several plays. While he has appeared before the public in the spectacular role of manager for Jane Cowl, for eight years he has been quietly and unobtrusively training himself to the business of the theatre by learning, and I mean really learning, just how the theatre works. He has a future, and whatever he does in it will be done, I feel sure, with intelligence and understanding, because he knows that the hit-or-miss methods of the past are no longer any good.

But even if he were to do nothing more, he will have the satisfaction of knowing that he has added to the sum total of our knowledge of a difficult and complicated problem. Speaking for myself, I would buy this book — and pay full price for it — if I weren't pretty sure that between the author and the publisher I'm going to get an editorial copy.

BARRETT H. CLARK

CONTENTS

TO THE UNINITIATED vii

FOREWORD ix

SECTION I · SO YOU WANT TO BE AN ACTOR? 1

How do you start? How do you get your first job? What is a casting agent? Where do you get information about casting? How do you "make the rounds"? Is there any accepted "system" of acting on Broadway? What do you do when you enter an office? What is the best time of the year to get a job? What salary will you earn? What is Actors' Equity? Are you sure of your job after you sign a contract? How about understudying? How about stock companies? How can you get to know people in the theatre? How long should you keep on trying? What opportunity is there for an actor outside of New York?

SECTION II · SO YOU WANT TO BE A PLAYWRIGHT? 35

Is it necessary to come to New York to sell a play? How do you market a play? What are the advantages of having an agent? What does the agent do for a playwright? What does an agent charge? Will an agent accept your play? Who are the best-known agents? What is the Dramatists' Guild? What are the fees and dues? What is the Minimum Basic Agreement? What advance does the author receive on selling a play? On what basis are royalties calculated? How much does a successful playwright earn? Does a successful playwright continue to be successful? What share does the playwright receive of a picture sale? What are the obligations of a producer to a playwright? What happens if a dispute arises between playwright and producer? What is the "negotiator"? What is a "play doctor"? What arrangement does the "play doctor" make? What may hold up production of your play after it has been bought? What about Amateur Rights? How important is casting in starting a production? Should you write a play for a star? What does it cost to produce a play? What is a renewal clause? Why does a play go on the road before a New York première? What are the advantages of a summer "try-out"? Are there any experimental theatres in New York? How does the Theatre Guild buy plays? How does the Group Theatre buy plays? How does the Theatre Union buy plays? Does a playwright make more money than a producer out of a successful play? How many playwrights are producers? Should a playwright direct his own play? Why do playwrights go to Hollywood?

Contents xv

SECTION III · SO YOU WANT TO BE A PRODUCER? 89

How do you become a producer? What does a producer do? How does a producer get started? How does a producer find a play? What is a play "worth" producing? What happens after a producer has read a play he likes? What does it cost to produce a play? How is a production budgeted? How is a "shoe-string" production budgeted? What are the items in the operating cost? What does the producer do during the production? How much does a producer make out of a success? What is the biggest hurdle in producing? How expressly do "rave" notices help a show? Do producers use their own money? How do you get backing? What does it cost to book a theatre? How much money can a producer make on tour? How does a producer share in picture rights? Is there any producers' association? Who have become producers? How many producers are there in New York? Is there room for more producers? What does it cost to maintain an office? What does a producer do when he is not producing?

SECTION IV · SO YOU WANT TO BE A DIRECTOR? 133

How do you get started? How does a director win a reputation? Who are the people who direct plays? How many producers direct their own productions? What producers do not direct their own productions? What salary does a director earn? When is a director paid? What kind of a contract does a director sign? Is there a directors' union? What is a director's relationship to a producer? Does a director supervise the lighting of a show? Are there any agents for directors? Does a director need experience as an actor? Should a director be able to rewrite a play? Does your age matter? What is a "director's holiday"? What does directing lead to?

SECTION V · SO YOU WANT TO BE A SCENE DESIGNER? 151

How do you begin as a scene designer? How do you join the union? What if a producer becomes interested in your work? What kind of a contract do you sign with a producer? What are the designer's duties? What does a scene designer earn? What are a scene designer's expenses? Can a scene designer paint his own scenery? Can a scene designer build his own scenery? How does the designer work with the director? What does designing in the theatre lead to?

SECTION VI · SO YOU WANT TO BE A STAGE MANAGER? 169

What does a stage manager do? How do you get a job as a stage manager? Do most directors

Contents

"carry" their own stage managers? What salary does a stage manager earn? Is a stage manager paid during rehearsals? Does a stage manager have to be an actor? Do stage managers have a union? What technical knowledge must a stage manager possess? How many jobs are there for stage managers? How many stage managers are there on Broadway? Do producers employ stage managers under long-term contract? What is the future in stage managing?

SECTION VII · SO YOU WANT TO BE A COMPANY MANAGER OR A PRESS AGENT? 183

What are a company manager's duties? What does a company manager earn? What are the duties of a press agent? What makes a "good" press agent? What does a press agent earn? How does a press agent get a job? Who are the best-known Broadway Press Agents? What experience do you need to become a press agent? What experience do you need to become a company manager? What does company managing or press agentry lead to?

SECTION VIII · SO YOU WANT TO BE A DRAMA CRITIC? 201

Where can you get a job as a drama critic? What other opportunities are there for drama *critics? What is the best kind of experience to become a drama critic? Of what value is a school of journalism course? What influence does a drama critic have? Why are critics sometimes attacked by producers? Do the New York critics know the people they write about? What are the advantages of reviewing an opening performance? What are the advantages of reviewing a second night performance? Do critics pay for their tickets? Are critics playwrights?*

SECTION IX · WHAT OPPORTUNITIES ARE THERE OUTSIDE OF NEW YORK? 217

What is a little theatre? What is a summer theatre? What are the leading little theatres? What are the leading summer theatres? How do you get a job in a summer theatre? What kind of jobs are there? Is a little theatre better than Broadway? How much money can you earn? Is there a chance to direct in a little theatre? To design? To build scenery? To paint scenery? Of what value is such experience in New York? Can you make a reputation in a little theatre? Can you make a reputation in a summer theatre? How much backing do you need to start a little or summer theatre? What openings are there with colleges and universities? Do you want to go into the theatre?

APPENDIX

BROADWAY GLOSSARY	243
NEW YORK PRODUCERS	247
NEW YORK PLAYBROKERS	250
NEW YORK CASTING AGENTS	252
SUMMER THEATRES	253
SUPPLEMENTARY READINGS	257

SECTION I

SO YOU WANT TO BE AN ACTOR?

"I suppose there will always be an opportunity of sorts for people bound for the stage, but I think we should be able and ought to try to make it a better regulated and more equitable arrangement than now exists."

— FRANK M. GILLMORE, *President of Actors' Equity Association, in a letter to the author*

"Hundreds of young people come to see me in my dressing room and ask me how they can get started in the theatre. I don't know what to say to them any more."

— GEORGE M. COHAN, *in conversation with the author*

SO YOU WANT TO BE AN ACTOR?

Answer: The only honest way to begin this book is to cite a few heartless statistics. There are approximately 8,400 actors in New York seeking employment. These figures are arbitrarily arrived at and probably are considerably short of the actual number of people who are to be found in New York seeking employment in the theatre as actors. According to Actors' Equity, that organization lists approximately 4,200 members, meaning that that many actors have appeared at one time or another professionally. It is very safe to add to this figure another 4,200 people who are trying to break in as actors, but have not yet secured their first professional engagement and, as a result, cannot belong to Equity.

Now for a few more grisly facts.

Of these 8,400 actors, Equity and non-Equity, approximately 2,000 appear before paying audiences each season. Each season there is a total of about 120 dramatic productions. Of these 120 productions, no more than 30 productions run over 20 weeks. In short, the actor who is employed 20 weeks a year has had extreme good luck, for either he has been fortunate enough to appear in a success, or else he has been able to obtain work in more than one play a season.

Of the total number of actors employed in the New York theatre each season, no more than 10% consist of those who are making their debut in the professional theatre. A simpler way of stating this is to say that out of 2,000 actors employed each season, approximately 200 get their first chance to act professionally, and of these 200 very few have the opportunity of playing a role any more important than a "bit."

The question of how much money these employed actors earn will come up a little later in this work. For the present, you may want to brood a bit on the foregoing facts.

HOW DO YOU START?

Answer: If you will be a realist, you should come to New York with sufficient money to live adequately for no less than six months and with the full understanding that during that entire period of time you are not likely to earn a red cent in the theatre. It is always possible that through some divine luck you may stumble into a job immediately, but it is nothing short of foolhardy to count on any such good fortune. The practical approach is to expect to spend at least six months before you are familiar with things along Broadway. You should also count on receiving at least some outside revenue for about a year after your arrival in New York.

As a matter of fact, it might be suggested that you will be much better off in general if you come into the theatre with a permanent independent income, so that your earnings as an actor need not concern you at all. . . .

Plan on it costing you no less than $25 a week to live, even though you lodge in modest quarters. Your room will cost about $9 a week if you stay at any sort of a hotel — and you must be where you have phone and message service, so a hotel it should be — food about $10; and carfares, cigarettes, phone calls, tailor, etc. will eat up the rest of your $25. That's just about rock bottom, if you are to have any freedom of mind.

You should be provided with a good wardrobe, especially if you are the female of the species. Broadway has a neat knack of sizing you up by your appearance. A young lady who walks into an office looking well-groomed and modishly attired will attract considerably more attention than plain Jane. Of course, if you really have talent, you can wear a pair of overalls and still act circles around a "clothes-horse". But you sometimes have a better chance to demonstrate that talent if you look impressive. Clothes make the woman is a legend that is singularly appropriate in the theatre.

If you are able to get letters of introduction to producers, fine, but don't expect those letters to work miracles for you or to get you a job. A letter of introduction will usually expedite an interview for you, but beyond that it is not likely to mean very much. Of course, a glowing letter about your rare talent, coming from someone whose judgment the producer happens to respect, can be valuable to you, but an ordinary letter of introduction will not do much more than cause a producer to receive you sooner than if you tried to reach him on your own.

If you can obtain letters of introduction to important people in the theatre, by all means do so. Anything that can possibly help you get a job is worth using. Personal introductions are always valuable in the theatre.

In brief, the answer as to how you are to start out is to know that you are financially equipped to look for a job and continue to look for it. Your confidence, your vitality, your freshness are your chief assets. If you are laboring under the strain that comes from worrying about money, you will be severely handicapped in the theatre. As the boys on the Main Stem say — come well-heeled.

HOW DO YOU GET YOUR FIRST JOB?

Answer: The race goes to the swift. When you go into the theatre you are entering active competition in a major sweepstake. Your competitors are all pitching pennies against thousand-dollar bills. The thing that drives them on is the constant hope of fame and fortune. Alertness of thought is coupled with luck, and the system is a vicious circle, as you shall see.

Bearing in mind that you will be one of thousands

So You Want to Be an Actor?

of actors looking for a job — 8,400 was the arbitrary figure quoted a bit earlier — and that the people who sit at the desks of producing offices become more than a little bored with the never-ceasing procession of actors that streams in and out of those offices each day, you have the key-note to your problem in getting started. Most of those faces somehow usually seem new to the people in the producing offices, so that the great war-cry is — "What have you done?"

They mean by that, have you had any experience and, if so, what? Have you been seen on Broadway?

If you are forced to say no to the latter question, that's where the vicious circle begins. You can't get a job on Broadway until you've had a job on Broadway! Well, what will help you get that elusive job on Broadway?

A casting agent can be of great help to you.

WHAT IS A CASTING AGENT?

Answer: A man or woman who has set up independent offices for the express purpose of helping producers cast their plays. Most of the established managers refer to these agents for assistance and advice.

Casting agents represent actors on three bases:

1. As straight employment agents, recommending you for a part in a single play, usually based on your "type" or a particular ability — perhaps the size of your physique or the color of your hair. You pay the agent

5% of your salary for a period of not more than 10 weeks, if the play runs that long.

2. As special employment representatives, securing for you a salary of no less than $125 a week and receiving 5% of your salary for the entire run of the play. Any agent who guarantees to get you a minimum salary of $125 a week must be convinced of your talent, obviously.

3. As personal representatives, guaranteeing you 20 weeks of work a season at no less than $100 a week and receiving a commission of 10% on your entire earnings. The personal representative acts as your business manager generally. To get this kind of representation you must be established in the theatre.

While there is an extended list of casting agents in the back of this book, there are several who more or less specialize in the casting of legitimate plays, as distinguished from those who give representation for other fields such as revues and musical comedies.

Among the agents who do the casting of a great many plays for producers are *Briscoe and Goldsmith,* 522 5th Avenue; *Jane Broder,* Times Building; *Chamberlain Brown,* 145 West 45th Street; *Sara Enright,* 234 West 44th Street; *Sylvia Hahlo,* 145 West 58th Street; *Max Hart,* 1560 Broadway; *William Liebling,* RKO Building, Rockefeller Center; *Maynard Morris,* 234 West 44th Street; *William Morris, Inc.,* RKO Building, Rockefeller Center; *Murray Phillips,* 755 7th Avenue; *Richard Pitman,* 1674 Broadway; *Louis Shurr,*

So You Want to Be an Actor?

Paramount Building; *Wales Winter,* 152 West 42nd Street; and *Georgia Wolfe,* 1493 Broadway.

It will now interest you to learn that no ranking agent in New York will represent an actor whose work he has not seen.

Having been to a producer who advises you to see an agent, you will follow his advice. You will go to an agent's office and be told to get a job first yourself and then let him know!

This will probably seem a little fantastic to you and yet, out of fairness to the agents, what other answer can they give you? They don't dare attempt to sell an unknown quantity to a producer who is in the business of producing plays precisely because it is a business, a very expensive and highly speculative business. A producer is always concerned with reducing his risk. Pity the agent who sells him a "bust".

So you still are faced by the problem of how you are going to get your first job.

Your best chance is with the producers. You will have to haunt the producing offices until you can persuade someone that you have ability and that you deserve a chance, even though it may be only a tiny one.

The three people, outside of a casting agent, who have a direct voice in the casting of a play are the producer, the director, and the playwright. Many producers direct their own plays. A listing of these producer-directors is given elsewhere in this book.

Producers usually keep their production plans a secret for the very reason that they dread having their offices bombarded with actors.

WHERE DO YOU GET INFORMATION ABOUT CASTING?

Answer: There are several sources where you can learn what is going on in the Broadway producing offices:

1. Read the trade papers — *Variety* and *Billboard*. Both these publications have expert reporters who sleuth down advance information.

2. The *New York Sunday Times* has a good drama page with a feature column called "Gossip of the Rialto" which frequently contains "inside" information obtained by an arch drama-reporter named Sam Zolotow. The *New York Sunday Herald-Tribune* also runs a detailed drama page.

3. There is also a service known as *"Zolotow's Guide",* a mimeographed booklet, published weekly and edited by the ace of the *New York Times,* containing a mass of detailed advance information on proposed productions. This service costs about $50 a year.

4. *Cliff Self,* a former actor, maintains a cubby-hole office at 1547 Broadway as an information bureau and charges a small weekly fee for his "dope".

5. The daily metropolitan papers all run drama columns.

It should be remarked that all these various drama reporters are constantly straining for news to fill up their columns. Their zeal to obtain information sometimes leads to pure guesswork and producers are frequently surprised to discover in print that they are planning productions of plays they have never even read! Then, too, many producers give information to these reporters for private reasons of their own that have no connection with actual production plans. In short, you can't always believe what you read.

But, with whatever information you obtain through these sources, you proceed to "make the rounds".

HOW DO YOU "MAKE THE ROUNDS"?

Answer: You can visit all the producing offices in town in about four hours, provided you are not kept waiting in any one office. You must be prepared, however, to do a great deal of waiting around in offices, particularly when you know a play is being cast for production. Actors know that they must cool their heels in offices to be interviewed.

You can visit the producing offices in a systematic way which will partially relieve wear and tear on your shoes and energies. The following itinerary for "making the rounds" will be helpful:

1. Begin with the Empire Theatre Building which is located at 40th Street and Broadway. Don't start out before eleven in the morning, because producing offices rarely begin to function earlier — at least for purposes of interviewing actors. In the Empire Theatre Building you will find located:

(a) *Sidney Harmon,* a young producer who has tremendous energy, never directs his own plays, sees practically everyone, always is planning a dozen different productions but produces only one or two plays a season.

(b) *Henry Forbes,* a middle-aged gentleman, who has a leaning toward producing "good" plays but who frequently does "money-makers"; he has encouraged many new young actors.

(c) *Walter Hart,* another young producer, who is also a very able director, interested in talented young actors, but finds it difficult to select the kind of plays he wants to produce.

(d) *Harry Moses,* a very sound business man who produces plays lavishly and well — his wife, Mrs. Elsa Moses, does most of the casting.

(e) *James Ullman,* a young producer, formerly associated with Sidney Harmon and now producing independently, soft-spoken and easy to talk with, is always glad to see new faces.

(f) *Irving Cooper,* also a young producer, has done very little thus far, engages free-lance directors, and likes to talk to new people, but is frank when he says he doesn't know when he will produce another play.

(g) *Jed Harris,* the stormy petrel of Broadway, an extremely gifted director, a man of variable moods, he may receive you pleasantly or he may be ruthlessly brief; he has an amazing gift for shrewd casting and

So You Want to Be an Actor? 13

has a knack for discovering fine actors; frequently difficult to see, since his office hours are irregular.

2. From the Empire Theatre, proceed to 42nd Street, West of 7th Avenue, where you visit first the New Amsterdam Theatre Building in which are located the offices of:

(a) *Max Gordon,* Broadway's most prolific and most lavish producer; he seldom sees actors, since his casting is done largely by free-lance directors; he is inclined toward using well-known actors in his productions — Ben Boyar, his general manager, Eddie Sobol, stage assistant, and Robert Sinclair, general stage director, should be sought out in this office.

(b) *George Kondolf,* a young man who produces infrequently and who is inclined to seeing few actors he does not already know.

(c) *S. M. Chartock,* also a young man who occasionally produces a play, but who makes no special plea for reputation in an actor's background.

3. From the New Amsterdam, go next door to 220 West 42nd Street where you will find:

(a) *George Abbott,* a very shrewd and clever producer-director with an illustrious record of smash hits, he casts to "type" and uses many unknowns; retains actors for several plays once he knows their work.

(b) *Joseph Bickerton,* attorney and "negotiator" for the Dramatists Guild, has occasionally produced plays and is sometimes silently connected with productions, having been Elmer Rice's partner at one time; a considerate and even-tempered man who will see actors occasionally. (Mr. Bickerton has since died.)

(c) *Charles Harris* is located at 226 West 42nd Street, a former general-manager for several producers, he is now interested in producing plays himself.

4. Go across the street to the Selwyn Theatre Building where you will find:

(a) *Crosby Gaige,* one of the best-established producers, a man of taste who produces both "good" and "commercial" plays, he can be seen by appointment through his general manager, Mack Hilliard.

(b) *Leonard Sillman,* a young producer who has confined his efforts to the musical field but who is also interested in legitimate plays.

(c) *Herman Shumlin,* one of Broadway's most astute producer-directors, formerly associated with Jed Harris and often unpredictable as to mood, he sees hundreds of actors, is very deliberate when casting a play, goes into production when he is convinced that everything is in good shape.

5. Next go two blocks up 8th Avenue to 44th Street. In the Lincoln Hotel, (a) *John Golden,* one of the oldest-established producers, he is hard to see — Dixie French, his general-manager, frequently recommends actors to him.

(b) Go East on 44th Street to the St. James Theatre which shelters *Eddie Dowling,* the former song-and-

So You Want to Be an Actor? 15

dance star who has turned play-producer; frequently tests his plays in summer theatres and will give young actors a chance.

(c) *The Group Theatre,* an organization of actor-managers interested in plays with social implications, they have enjoyed great success along Broadway; difficult to break in with them, they follow a dialectic in acting that derives from Stanislawski's method — membership begins with Cheryl Crawford, Harold Clurman and Lee Strasberg, all of whom are directors.

6. Next door to the St. James is the Little Theatre where:

(a) *Brock Pemberton* makes his office, produces infrequently but usually with success, and interviews people regularly even when not producing — his partner and co-director is Antoinette Perry, a charming and gifted woman who is rarely in the office.

Adjoining the Little Theatre is the Sardi Building at 234 West 44th Street where *Lawrence Schwab* is to be found. He usually does musical shows but sometimes produces plays; casts to type occasionally but prefers well-known players.

7. Leaving the Sardi Building, cross the street and enter the Shubert Theatre where you will find (a) *Lee Shubert's* office on the second floor; he makes it a practise to see everyone who visits him, if only for a few seconds, you do not have to be announced but merely wait until he appears at the door of his office and

beckons to you; his organization is a vast realty-holding company and he produces more plays each season than any other manager; he has an amazing memory for faces and young people, he seems cold at first, but is always interested in talent — on the floor above is his nephew (b) *Milton Shubert,* a young man, who is general manager of the firm and produces many of the Shubert plays personally.

8. Walk through Shubert Alley which connects 44th Street with 45th Street and enter the Plymouth Theatre. On the balcony-landing of that theatre (a) *Arthur Hopkins* has his office, he sees everyone, rarely talks to an actor, lets you do all the talking, and, if he likes your looks, will say to come back the next day for rehearsal if he is doing a show! One of the most respected of all producer-directors, he is always in his office during the morning.

Across the Street from the Plymouth is the Music Box Theatre and on the balcony-landing there you will find (b) *Sam Harris* who is associated with George S. Kaufman, and who is one of the most successful producers in the professional theatre; he can be seen by appointment and is a little hard of hearing, but very shrewd in discovering new talent — Morris Jacobs is his general manager and does most of the preliminary interviewing.

9. Go down Broadway to 44th Street again and turn East. In the Hudson Theatre, now known as the Co-

So You Want to Be an Actor? 17

lumbia Broadcasting System Playhouse, you will find *William Harris, Jr.,* a producer who has been in the theatre for many years and been extremely successful, he directs his own plays usually, does not like "dull" people, has been known to take a chance on obscure actors in important roles.

At 19 West 44th Street, you will find located the offices of a producing firm known as *Laurence Rivers, Inc.,* which is headed by Rowland Stebbins, an ex-Wall Street broker, who has produced several distinguished plays — Charles Stewart is his general manager, and Miriam Doyle does most of the casting and directing.

10. Walk up 6th Avenue to 47th Street and visit the Playhouse Theatre on that street where you will find the offices of:

(a) *William A. Brady, Sr.,* the well-known showman, who ranks as a pioneer in the professional theatre, kindly, sympathetic with youngsters, a sharp business-man, difficult to see because he is frequently out of New York.

(b) *Dwight Deere Wiman,* a young society-man, who has carved out an enviable reputation in the theatre as a successful manager, very rarely in his office and can be seen only by appointment — Forest Haring is his general manager and interviews actors at appointed hours.

(c) *George Bushar and John Tuerk,* a recently formed producing firm with ambitious plans; Tuerk has been associated with many productions in the past and interviews actors by appointment, a shrewd man, inclined to being brief with new people.

11. Go back to 6th Avenue to the RKO Building which is located at 1270 6th Avenue. Here you will find the offices of:

(a) *Guthrie McClintic,* distinguished producer-director who is always interested in new people, extremely courteous and tolerant, frequently gives actors their first Broadway part — Stanley Gilkie is his general-manager and grants preliminary interviews.

(b) *Katharine Cornell* is located in the McClintic office, since he is her husband — her productions are all managed by the McClintic staff, so she is rarely in the office.

(c) *Al Woods,* veteran producer, who is always willing to see a new actor, since he claims all the stars have gone to Hollywood and he must help find new ones. He asks disconcerting questions and warms up quickly when he believes you have talent. His secretary, Miss Levy, arranges his appointments.

12. Walk West on 52nd Street and between Broadway and 8th Avenue you will find the Guild Theatre where the *Theatre Guild* is located. Theresa Helburn and Philip Moeller supervise most of the casting for their organization.

13. Scattered about in various buildings in the Broadway district are a number of other producers for

So You Want to Be an Actor?

you to visit, including Gilbert Miller, Vinton Freedley, Frederick Ayer, Alex Yokel, Theron Bamberger, and others whose names and addresses you will discover in the back of this book.

This completes a fair sample of "making the rounds". Of course, each season, new producers are constantly springing up and dropping out of the Broadway scene. Each producer requires a different approach and you must keep your wits sharp when you are being interviewed.

The nice part about the whole business of looking for a job as an actor, is that, since it is not likely that you have read the play which the producer has on his desk, you do not have the vaguest idea whether the manuscript is any good or whether there is a part in it that you can play. When "making the rounds" you will hear frequently, "There's nothing in it for you!"

And that means you're not the type!

IS THERE ANY ACCEPTED "SYSTEM" OF ACTING ON BROADWAY?

Answer: If you are interested in the art of acting from the view-point of an accepted acting tradition, such as may be found in the Comédie Française in Paris or with the Moscow Art Theatre Company, there is no such tradition in the Broadway theatre.

If there is any pronounced method of acting at all on Broadway, it is the realistic style of acting, based on "type casting". Producers and directors usually size up an actor according to his appearance and personality, in order to bring a convincing and "real" character to a production.

Broadway productions rehearse for only a few weeks. As a result, there is never much time to devote to discussions of acting theory or technique in the fully rounded sense. Again, an actor who is unknown to the management has only seven days of rehearsal in which to prove his aptitude for a role. None of which leads to profound discussion during rehearsals. You simply do your job and do it as well as you know how, instinctively and with whatever assistance the director, or sometimes the playwright, will offer you.

Only great stars, or important featured players, will take time out of a rehearsal to sit down and discuss the theory of a performance.

The Group Theatre acting company, composed of young people who are definitely seeking new rich methods in the theatre, employ an adapted method of the Moscow Art Theatre Company theory of acting, but they are very much alone in seeking a distinctive acting technique along Broadway.

Another point for you to bear in mind about the Broadway theatre is that the ultimate goal of every actor is to appear in a "hit". "Hits" run for a long time. Playing the same part in a play, night after night, week after week, can become deadly monotonous. Yet, it's the kind of engagement every actor strives to win.

WHAT DO YOU DO WHEN YOU ENTER AN OFFICE?

Answer: Be yourself.

There is nothing that annoys producers and their assistants so much as the actor who gives an "office performance". Don't try to be something you are not in normal life. Remember, most producers cast to type and your type may be exactly what is wanted. Producers are chary of artificiality and they are bored and even annoyed by "office acting". The best you can hope to achieve from "doing an act" in a producer's office is to amuse him. Be enthusiastic, if that is your normal temperament, or be reticent, if that is how you feel. At all times be direct. In short, be yourself.

Try to impress yourself on the producer's secretary when you are trying to see him and be sure the secretary gets to know you. Frequently, you will find the producer cannot be seen. If you can't get an appointment with him the first time, come again and again. Or, better yet, write a brief note mentioning that you have tried to see him and ask for an appointment.

Don't be discouraged when you are told there is no casting. The chief problem of the producer is to find a manuscript he thinks worthy of producing. There are long stretches of time when he does nothing but read plays. It's a good time to see a producer when he's not casting a play — he may remember you when he does get busy.

Usually producers are interested in interviewing new people, particularly if they find some vitality in the subject of the interview. Try to get to know the producers personally and visit them repeatedly until you have made a distinct impression. When entering an office, try to feel confident and remember that a producer is only a human being like yourself. If you have something to say, the chances are he'll meet you on your own ground.

Make sure your name, address and telephone number are with every office in town and follow up regularly every contact you make in an office. And continue to be yourself.

WHEN IS THE BEST TIME OF THE YEAR TO GET A JOB?

Answer: Activity in the theatre is distinctly seasonal. Producers try to gauge when audiences are likely to patronize plays, since a paying audience is what makes the wheels go around in the theatre.

There is always a rush of productions coming into New York during the months of September, October and November, which is considered the beginning of the season. Casting for these productions begins during the month of August and continues most heavily till the middle of September.

During December, there is a lull in casting activities because of the holidays.

Activity picks up after the holidays and continues

So You Want to Be an Actor?

until the lull that attends business during Lent. After Easter there is a brief spell of activity and the season is practically over in May, or as soon as there is a feeling of warm weather in the air.

There are producers, however, who pay small attention to seasonal matters and who believe a good play will succeed at any time of the year. Usually something always is stirring in a producing office, particularly if there is a worthy manuscript on hand, since producers often plan a production months ahead. But the large bulk of producing is done from the beginning of September until the end of December, excluding the beginning of December. The balance of production comes from the middle of January through April. There are very few late Spring productions. July is almost completely inactive.

WHAT SALARY WILL YOU EARN?

Answer: Anyone who takes up a career should expect to make a living out of his work. The question of salary for actors in the theatre defies explanation, since it is calculated on an arbitrary scale. The most famous of actors will set what he considers his "salary" and then will take whatever the traffic will bear, unless he is so secure that he can demand his price.

A star may demand and get $1,000 or $1,500 a week plus a percentage of the weekly gross, or perhaps work on a split salary and percentage of the weekly gross receipts, or on a straight percentage of the gross. There are one or two top-ranking stars, whose box-office value cannot be questioned by a producer, who demand and get $1,500 a week, plus a percentage of the weekly gross, plus a percentage of the net profits on the production.

Don't be dazzled by those figures. Examine what goes before you become a star.

A featured or well-known player may earn between $200 and $750 a week, although the tendency in the commercial theatre today is to reduce the salaries of featured players.

An actor playing a small but important part may earn between $100 and $150 a week.

Examine these figures only in terms of being an established actor and remember that very few plays run for any length of time and that even a well-known actor does not work in much more than one or two plays each season.

The important thing to remember is that you are not likely to receive any such salary at the beginning. There are two minimum basic salaries that concern you directly. These two minimum levels are $40 a week for what Actors' Equity terms Senior Members and $25 a week for Junior Members. You will fall into the latter classification.

Approximately 2,000 actors receive employment in legitimate plays each season. (There are still a few

So You Want to Be an Actor?

touring productions each season which may provide work for a few hundred other actors.) There are about 120 dramatic productions of new plays each season in the professional New York theatre. (In some cases, foreign productions are imported bodily with either their entire original casts or their principal actors.) Of these 120 productions, approximately 82% are failures, running anywhere from one night to three or four weeks, the majority of them closing within one or two weeks.

Out of the 2,000 actors who are employed during a season, approximately 1,400 appear in failures and work for an average of about six weeks a year.

The average income for these 1,400 actors is between $150 and $600 a year, or $2.88 to $12 a week!

It's perfectly true that those are average figures, based on the run-of-the-mine salary and success of an actor. But it's the only intelligent way of examining the situation. To do better, you must have extraordinary talent and dazzling luck. How talented are you? How lucky?

According to Emily Holt of Actors' Equity, between 5% and 10% of all the members of that association earn enough money to live adequately and save for the future.

Finally, just as the producer is forced to aim for a smash hit or nothing, you, as an actor, are faced with the same outlook. In order to earn a living in the theatre, you have to be on top of the heap! There is no middle strata.

WHAT IS ACTORS' EQUITY?

Answer: This is a union of actors which you must join, *once you are employed in a professional production.* Equity was formed in 1917 for the protection of actors and to assure them certain basic rights. Of the approximate number of 8,400 actors looking for employment in New York, already quoted, half of that number are members of Equity. The others have not yet secured their first job.

If you are visited by Dame Fortune and finally get a job, before you go into rehearsal with the play, pay a visit to the office of Actors' Equity Association at 45 West 47th Street and make application for membership. You will then be considered for Junior Membership and passed on by the Equity Council, a board elected each year. The initiation fee is $50 and the yearly dues are $18. You become a Senior Member automatically after you have worked in the theatre for two years.

If you find it inconvenient to pay your $50 initiation fee immediately, you can go to the producer of the play for which you have been engaged and ask him to pay it for you, since the producer is obliged to engage an all-Equity cast of actors. The producer will probably take your I.O.U. for $50 and deduct it from your salary on pay day which falls on the first Saturday afternoon after the play has opened.

Actors' Equity guarantees its members that they will be paid two weeks' salary by the producer who is required to post a bond with Equity covering these salaries for the cast. For this two weeks' salary, you are required to rehearse for four weeks, although a producer often rehearses for only three weeks. Occasionally a producer receives special permission from Equity to rehearse for five weeks when the production is elaborate.

A new ruling has been effected by Equity recently whereby the actor receives what is termed "expense money" during the rehearsal period. For the first week of rehearsal you receive nothing. But for the second and third weeks, Junior Members are entitled to $15 a week and Senior Members to $20 a week. The producers are at liberty to retire this amount of money from the bond, so that if the play is closed within two weeks after its opening performance, you still will receive a total of only two weeks' salary, as contracted. However, if the producer rehearses for more than three weeks, then you receive additional "expense money" each week of rehearsal, which may not be deducted from the bond. If the producer rehearses beyond the period allowed by Equity, full salary must be paid to the cast even though the play is not yet being performed before a paying audience.

The gist of this is that you may rehearse in a play for three weeks and play for two weeks, a total of five weeks, and receive for your entire efforts two weeks' salary! If you are a Junior Member and receiving the minimum scale of $25 weekly, which is highly likely, you will earn exactly $50. And it will cost you that much to join Equity!

ARE YOU SURE OF YOUR JOB AFTER YOU SIGN A CONTRACT?

Answer: No.

The standard and lengthy Equity contract that the producer signs with an actor gives the producer the right to keep an actor in rehearsal for seven days without any obligation on his part. The producer has those seven days of rehearsal in which to determine whether you are suited to the part. He can release you without obligation on the seventh day or earlier.

If, for any reason, you are released after the period of seven days, the producer is obligated to pay you two weeks' salary as contracted. You may think you are doing well even during the last week of rehearsing in a play and be released by the producer, for various reasons, by his paying you two weeks' salary immediately.

You can also be released from a play after it has opened, particularly when the play is given an out-of-town try-out. (Transportation back is guaranteed.) The manager, in this case, can release you by giving you a written two weeks' notice or two weeks' salary immediately. But you have the same privilege of leaving the company by either rendering to the producer two weeks' notice or by paying him your contracted salary for two weeks immediately. Frequently an actor may wish to leave a company to accept a better engagement. It is customary in this case to submit notice.

WHAT ABOUT UNDERSTUDYING?

Answer: Almost all companies have understudies. In many cases, however, the producer does not go to this expense until the play is open and its success is determined.

The understudy is paid arbitrarily according to the number of parts assigned to cover. Salary may range from the minimum of $25 a week to $100 a week, rarely more, unless you are playing a "bit" and understudying several important roles as well.

The understudy must appear at the theatre at each performance a half hour before curtain time and report to the stage-manager.

The value of understudying is that you can get experience and that you may possibly go on one night in the place of an actor who is indisposed or who decides to leave the cast. You also make a contact with a producing office in this fashion and you may receive a part in the next production.

When you are looking for a job, remember that understudying is a good start. If a producer seems reluctant to give you a big part, but seems interested in you, ask for the chance of understudying. Many well-known actors began this way.

WHAT ABOUT STOCK COMPANIES?

Answer: In the old days, before the advent of talking pictures, there was a stock company in practically every important town in the country. It was a constant testing ground for actors. But the bottom has dropped out of the business and there are only about a dozen stock companies of any importance left in the country. These companies are inclined to engage well-known actors rather than tyros. Guest-stars are often used, too. And in addition, there are thousands of ex-stock favorites to be drawn from, men and women who used to make a good living in stock who are now haunting New York for work.

Mr. Lane of Actors' Equity is well-acquainted with what little activity still exists in stock companies and may be approached at the Equity office for information, since the field is a fluctuating one.

The fact that you have played in stock, however, means very little to a Broadway producer or to casting agents, unless you can persuade one of them to pay your theatre a visit should you get a job in stock. The chances of either happening are slim.

HOW CAN YOU GET TO KNOW PEOPLE IN THE THEATRE?

Answer: The Broadway world is actually very small,

So You Want to Be an Actor?

although much of the foregoing has probably seemed terrifying and vast. When you first arrive in New York, the theatre will seem a complicated maze, but it will soon become familiar. While going the rounds you will strike up acquaintances with actors, for one thing. Actors are always helpful in telling you what is going on around town, since this is a reciprocal function. You will find little groups of them everywhere around Broadway, in the Shubert Alley, on the corner of 45th Street and 7th Avenue, in front of the Bond Building on 7th Avenue, outside of offices, at the Lambs Club and the Players Club, if you are a member of those actors' clubs, at the Equity offices, etc. Actors are a fraternal lot as a whole and there is a camaraderie among them.

There are other well-known rendezvous for people in the theatre that should be mentioned. The first is Sardi's Restaurant where you can lunch for about a dollar and where many important people of the theatre are to be found. If you have a friend who can introduce you to people, you may make valuable connections there.

Then there is "Tony's" and "Twenty One" on 52nd Street, West of 5th Avenue, both late spots, where many prominent theatre folk gather to gossip.

"Ralph's" on 45th Street, West of Broadway, and "The Eat Shop" around the corner from "Ralph's" on 8th Avenue, are two restaurants patronized by people of the theatre. The Piccadilly Hotel Drug Store and The Penn-Astor Drug Store on 45th Street, and Walgreen's Drug Store in the Paramount Building are frequented by many people of the theatre.

You can often find out what's "going on" by chatting with people in these places.

Crass as it may seem, making social connections in the theatre are helpful — providing you have talent to back it all up.

HOW LONG SHOULD YOU KEEP ON TRYING?
Answer: Few of you probably want to ask that question, yet it should be answered after a fashion, even though one gulps a little in formulating a comprehensive response.

Try and remember this, if you can. Do not confuse the urge with the talent. You may feel deeply and passionately that you have all the makings of a great actor. You may burn with ardor to act. You may feel sure because something is gnawing at your vitals to act that inevitably you will be an actor. It doesn't follow. You may be wrong. You may not have the stuff of an actor in you at all, no matter how pleased they were with you in your college dramatic society plays.

If you haven't been able to get a job at the end of a year, even though you may have "read" for producers or even rehearsed in a play, only to be released, don't be discouraged, if you still believe in yourself. There are many actors, who are well-known today, who went for one or two years without getting a job at all. But if you do get work and find at the end of two years that you are not making any progress in the theatre, then take time out for a careful look at yourself. It may be high time for you to quit and try something else in which you are more likely to succeed. Try to be your own critic, when you can, and also ask a director, whom you respect and whom you have worked for, to tell you frankly what he thinks of your ability. You can make a living out of acting only if you have talent and if that talent attracts attention.

And, in conclusion, if you have talent, nine times out of ten it is *recognized* after you have served a proper period of apprenticeship. Very few really talented actors go unrecognized forever. A good actor may not work consistently but at least it will be common knowledge that he *is* a good actor.

If you spend several years in the theatre and no one seems to recognize you, something is probably wrong with your talent.

WHAT OPPORTUNITY IS THERE FOR AN ACTOR OUTSIDE OF NEW YORK?

Answer: There are several excellent little theatres and there are also the summer theatres. These are discussed under a separate heading in this book.

SECTION II

SO YOU WANT TO BE A PLAYWRIGHT?

"The theatre is by far the most precarious field of activity for a writer in that from the box-office point of view there is no such thing as an established author. A novelist or magazine writer will, assuming progressive ability, make an increasingly profitable reputation. But however many successes a dramatist may have, his next play can always be a 'flop'!"

— ADRIENNE MORRISON, *prominent literary agent, in a note to the author*

SO YOU WANT TO BE A PLAYWRIGHT?

Answer: Anyone who creates a group of characters on paper and confines those characters in some sort of a story or situation expressed entirely through dialogue meant for actors to speak before an audience, interrupting that story or situation by act or scene divisions, can call himself a playwright!

It is not the purpose of this text to give instruction in the technique of playwriting, any more than it is to teach the methods of acting or scene designing.

For the purposes of this book, the correct answer to the above question is to impart specific information for the benefit of anyone who has written or intends to write a play and who does not know what practical steps to take after that.

It is possible that the best thing for you to do with your manuscript is to hide it or burn it, for all the good it will do you or anyone else. But that is not the true problem at hand, only the final one.

No one can stop you from writing a play and no one can deprive you of the pleasure or agony obtained from writing it.

IS IT NECESSARY TO COME TO NEW YORK TO SELL A PLAY?

Answer: No.

The playwright is one person in the theatre who does not have to be on hand to sell his wares.

In order for an actor to get a job in the theatre, he has to present himself to a producer both to be seen and heard. A scene designer can explain his drawings to a producer. A technician can discuss his ideas and "sell" himself. A press agent can display his wares by his personality. Practically every worker in the theatre can help himself land a job in the theatre through his sheer physical presence and delivery.

But not a playwright.

The playwright's stock in trade is his manuscript, which must be *read* to be evaluated. Either the producer likes what he reads or he doesn't. No amount of haranguing or explanation from the playwright in person can have any effect, one way or the other, *at the beginning*.

Once the producer has read your play, he may want to discuss it with you, certainly. But that's another story. The point is you do not have to deliver your manuscript in person in order to get it read.

In short, there is no reason for a playwright to come to New York. There is no harm in bringing your play in person to a producer, but, by the same token, there is no practical good to be gained from it.

So You Want to Be a Playwright?

HOW DO YOU MARKET A PLAY?

Answer: There are two methods.

Either you can mail or bring your play to the producer direct, or you can entrust it to an agent.

The disadvantages of the former method are more or less obvious. You have no notion of what the producer is looking for, if anything. You know nothing about his financial condition, his talent, his taste, or his personality. Similarly he knows nothing about you or, more important, your play.

In short, trying to sell a play yourself is difficult, particularly if you are not familiar with the producers and if you are unknown and without any reputation as a writer.

WHAT ARE THE ADVANTAGES OF HAVING AN AGENT?

Answer: Even the established authors, who have had more than one production, usually employ agents, or playbrokers, as they are sometimes called, to transact their business for them.

Of direct concern to you is the fact that the number of plays that are sold without an agent making the preliminary negotiations is not large.

For one thing, the Broadway producers have come to rely heavily on the agents to supply them with manuscripts suited to their needs and tastes. Most of the agents know their customers, the producers, personally, and know how to approach them with a play.

They may know what producer will be interested in your particular play. Again, an agent who has handled several successful plays acquires a definite reputation and his manuscripts are given careful and prompt attention by the producers.

The agent not only paves the way for the sale of a play through an enthusiastic approach, but he also transacts all the business arrangements that attend and follow the sale for an author. He arranges all the details of the author's contract with the producer, collects all royalties promptly, and at all times represents the author in any situation that may arise with the producer.

While producers are usually ready to read, or have read for them, practically any manuscript that finds its way into their offices, the usual approach to the reading of an unsolicited manuscript is that it is probably worthless.

The producer knows that an agent has already weeded out some of the wheat from the chaff.

As a result, the producer, knowing that a manuscript coming to him from an agent has already passed at least one more or less acid test, will give it more than casual attention. An agent does not handle a play unless he thinks it has some merit and sales possibility, for he is in business to *sell* plays. This does not mean that an agent believes fervently that every play he handles is a potential gold mine. Frequently, an agent is convinced that the author of a manuscript has talent and deserves a hearing and chance to be "built up", and will handle a play to make the author at least known to producers.

WHAT DOES THE AGENT DO FOR A PLAYWRIGHT?

Answer: The agent acts generally as a sales-force, as already indicated.

Specifically, the agent is obligated to protect the author and to see that the contract between the author and the producer is adhered to.

The agent not only assumes the responsibility of collecting and forwarding the author's royalties weekly, but may also represent the author in matters of casting, direction, billing and rewriting. It is the agent's specific duty to protect the author's property and to advise him on everything pertaining to production and business.

Most agents also represent the author for motion pictures and negotiate contracts that take the author to Hollywood. Agents frequently obtain for their clients commissions to execute adaptations and "play-doctoring" assignments for producers requiring such services.

An agent is the author's representative, in the full sense of the word.

WHAT DOES AN AGENT CHARGE?

Answer: In exchange for his services, the agent receives

10% of the author's gross earnings, including royalties derived from a sale of motion picture rights, foreign production, radio, stock, etc. This also includes 10% of the advance payment of royalties received by the author on the initial sale of the play.

A few agents charge what is called a "reading fee" of several dollars before they will examine an unsolicited and unrecommended manuscript, but, as a rule, most agents will read free of charge any play they receive, in the hope of finding a marketable manuscript.

WILL AN AGENT ACCEPT YOUR PLAY?

Answer: Not if he doesn't like it. And that means not if he is positive he cannot sell it.

Maintaining any sort of an office costs money and no agent wants to burden himself with the unnecessary expense and effort of trying to merchandise a play that he feels has no sales value.

If an agent does not like your play, he will send it back to you, probably collect. In most cases, the agent will not send you any detailed opinion of what he thinks is wrong with your play, unless he is interested in the manuscript and is returning it to you for revisions that he thinks are necessary.

Again, once an agent has accepted your play and tried to sell it over a period of time with no success, he will return the play to you and explain that he has been unable to dispose of it for you.

Acceptance of your manuscript by an agent is far

from a guarantee that it will be sold. An agent can only *try* to sell your play. His enthusiasm for your play may not be shared by a producer.

WHO ARE THE BEST-KNOWN AGENTS?

Answer: This question can be answered only in terms of specific achievements. A complete list of the better-known agents in the business of selling plays appears in the back of this work.

The following agents are commonly considered important by producers:

Allied Authors Agency, 229 West 42nd Street, a recently formed agency, headed by Alexander Sukennikoff and Lester Sweyd. This firm represents Helen Jerome, the author of "Pride and Prejudice", among others.

American Play Company, 33 West 42nd Street. John Rumsey is the president of the firm and devotes himself personally to the management of the play department. In recent years, this was one of the most powerful agencies in selling successful plays, having marketed such manuscripts as "Fair and Warmer", "Rain", "The High Road", etc. Mr. Rumsey complains bitterly these days of a lack of talented new authors and is very eager to find good manuscripts. But he will handle only those plays which he feels have exceptional merit.

Brandt & Brandt, 101 Park Avenue. Harold Freedman and Janet Cohn, his assistant, handle the play department of his agency which is one of the largest in the business. The firm represents such authors as Robert Sherwood, S. N. Behrman, Maxwell Anderson, Clifford Odets, John Howard Lawson, Cecil Holm, George Abbott, etc., and has had an enormously successful record with such plays as "The Petrified Forest", "Rain from Heaven", "Three Men on a Horse", etc. They are rather "choosy" about the plays and authors they handle.

Curtis Brown, Inc., 18 East 48th Street. An important British firm with a large office in New York. The firm represents both British and American authors.

Frieda Fishbein, 1482 Broadway. Miss Fishbein conducts a modest agency with great zeal. She is extremely interested in new authors. Miss Fishbein was the agent for Elmer Rice's "Street Scene" and Moss Hart's "Once in a Lifetime".

Samuel French, Inc., 25 West 45th Street. Until recently, Barrett H. Clark, the well-known critic and writer, handled the new play department for this agency, which is prominent for its publication of plays intended for amateur performance. Mr. Clark has blazed the way for many new experiments in the theatre and has espoused the cause of such authors as Paul Green, George O'Neil, E. P. Conkle, Albert Bein, Lynn Riggs, John Wexley, Michael Blankfort, Leopold Atlas, etc., all of whom have been represented by this firm.

Leland Hayward, Inc., 654 Madison Avenue. This

So You Want to Be a Playwright?

is a high-powered and very successful concern. Miriam Howell heads the play department and Mr. Hayward himself operates both in New York and in California where he is in close tabs with executives of the major motion picture companies. The firm represents such authors as Ben Hecht and Charles MacArthur, Corey Ford, Jack Kirkland, Russel Crouse, Albert Maltz and George Sklar, etc.

International Literary Bureau, 521 5th Avenue. Sanford Greenberger handles the plays for this concern. A "quality" firm which specializes more or less in importing British manuscripts. They are interested, however, in American playwrights.

Alice Kauser, 152 West 42nd Street. Miss Kauser has been a veteran playbroker for many years. She represents Zoe Akins, among others, and was responsible recently for the sale of "The Old Maid" and "I Loved You Wednesday".

Maxim Lieber, 545 5th Avenue. While Mr. Lieber is best known as a literary agent, he also handles a few selected play manuscripts. Among several other distinguished authors, he represents Erskine Caldwell from whose novel the play "Tobacco Road" was adapted.

Richard Madden, 33 West 42nd Street. Mr. Madden has an international reputation as the agent for Eugene O'Neill. He conducts his business quietly and efficiently and represents several notable authors, including Sean O'Casey, James Bridie and John Drinkwater.

Dr. Edmond Pauker, 1639 Broadway. Dr. Pauker is one of the leading agents of foreign plays, representing most of the best Continental authors, including Ferenc Molnar. He was the agent for the enormously successful "Grand Hotel". Is interested in American playwrights.

Pinker and Morrison, 9 East 46th Street. The play department is conducted by Adrienne Morrison who has been very successful as a playbroker. "The Last Mile" by John Wexley was one of her plays and recently she was represented by "Post Road", the "hit" play by Norma Mitchell and Wilbur Daniel Steele.

Leah Salisbury, 234 West 44th Street. Miss Salisbury, a most energetic woman, has sold such plays as "Gentlemen of the Press", "Ten Minute Alibi", "Young Love", "Accent on Youth", and "Boy Meets Girl". She is well connected with motion picture officials.

Ann Watkins, Inc., 210 Madison Avenue. Pat Duggan is in charge of the play department. A young man, he is wide awake and enterprising and interested in getting high prices for his clients. Mr. Duggan was the agent for Sidney Howard's adaptation of "Dodsworth" and for "Page Miss Glory" which attracted a large sum for its picture rights. He will not accept a play until he is convinced he can sell it.

Gertrude Workman, 117 East 10th Street. Miss Workman represents a few selected authors including Katharine Clugston, Courtenay Savage and Knowles Entrikin. Recently she sold an unproduced play by Katharine Clugston which was used as a starring talking-picture vehicle for George Arliss under the title of "The Last Gentleman".

Many literary agencies, specializing in merchandising the manuscripts of novels and stories, also handle plays. In addition, there are a host of individuals who crop up each season and become playbrokers.

An enterprising agent, no matter how slight his reputation, can win the attention of a producer with a good manuscript through virtue of the fact that he is in business as an agent. Consequently, the list of playbrokers already cited is not intended as a limited recommendation of the field, only as a representative one.

WHAT IS THE DRAMATISTS' GUILD?

Answer: The Dramatists' Guild, 9 East 38th Street, a branch of the Authors' League of America, Inc., is an organization formed by authors for their mutual protection. The Dramatists' Guild, in order to prevent natural abuses which may assail an author in the theatre, operates on what amounts to a closed shop basis. In essence, no playwright may have his play produced without becoming a member of the Guild. This is accomplished through a Minimum Basic Agreement between the Guild and the producing managers, whereby no manager may produce a play without having signed that general agreement.

A playwright is not eligible for membership in the Dramatists' Guild until he has sold a play.

In actual fact, however, there is nothing to prevent a producer from refusing to sign the Minimum Basic Agreement, except that he cannot produce plays by authors who are already members of the Guild. Similarly, he is at liberty, if he has not signed the agreement, to produce a play by an author who has not yet joined the Guild. It so happens that all the established playwrights are members of the Guild and a newcomer who does not want to join is more than a little foolish. The net result is that the Dramatists' Guild is a very powerful organization in the theatre.

WHAT ARE THE FEES AND DUES?

Answer: Briefly, an author is taxed a $10 initiation fee on becoming a member of the Dramatists' Guild once he has sold a play.

The minimum dues are $10 a year with assessments on the playwright's royalties up to gross royalties of $2,500 a year. The maximum dues are $250 a year.

WHAT IS THE MINIMUM BASIC AGREEMENT?

Answer: The Minimum Basic Agreement is a lengthy contract between the Dramatists' Guild and theatrical producing managers, defining in complete detail all the terms and conditions whereby a playwright sells his play to a producer.

So You Want to Be a Playwright? 49

The contract is extremely specific, designed to protect the author and his play equitably, and consumes almost 30 pages of closely printed legal matter.

No producer can present a play, in effect, until he has signed the agreement, without being subject to general boycott by the members of the Dramatists' Guild.

The contract allows for arbitration in all matters open to legitimate dispute between the author and producer.

The contract is referred to as a "minimum" agreement, because it defines the lowest terms on which a playwright may sell his play. The minimum, however, does not imply the maximum. The author is permitted to seek the highest terms the traffic will bear.

The contract is too lengthy to discuss in its entirety, but its major points will be explained in this work.

WHAT ADVANCE PAYMENT DOES THE AUTHOR RECEIVE ON SELLING A PLAY?

Answer: Until recently, the producer usually paid to the author advance royalties of $500 on buying an option to produce a play and for this sum owned the play for six months, although frequently the advance was considerably less, or even nothing.

A revision in the Minimum Basic Agreement by the Dramatists' Guild has changed this arrangement. Now the producer pays to the playwright $100 on signing a contract and for this sum controls the play for a period of one month. He is permitted to renew his option on the play each month for the next six months by paying to the author an additional $100 each month. At the end of six months he may renew his option monthly by additional payments of $150 each month. If he has not produced the play at the end of one year, all rights revert to the author.

All advance royalties are paid to the author through the Dramatists' Guild. This is done to protect the author against any "deal" a producer may try to make with him.

These payments are an advance against royalties and are deducted from the playwright's first royalties when the play is running before a paying audience, until the advance has been covered in full.

ON WHAT BASIS ARE ROYALTIES CALCULATED?

Answer: The author's royalties are always computed on the weekly gross receipts.

Formerly the Dramatists' Guild never listed any minimum royalty terms in the basic agreement between authors and producers, because they did not wish the minimum ever to become the maximum and because they wanted the author to be able to secure from the producer the highest terms the traffic would bear.

However, the commonly accepted minimum royalties in actual practise along Broadway have always

So You Want to Be a Playwright?

been what is referred to as "five, seven and a half, and ten." Recently these minimum terms were incorporated into the basic agreement as the lowest royalty terms a producer can make with an author.

Translated into figures, this means that the author receives 5% of the first $5,000 obtained at the box-office each week by the producer, 7½% of the next $2,000, and 10% on anything above that.

For example, let us say that a play takes in gross receipts of $10,000 a week.

On a $10,000 gross, the author's royalties are:

5% of the first $5,000 .... $250
7% of the next $2,000 150
10% of the remaining $3,000 300
                                   ─────
                                   $700 Total

Thus on the minimum royalty terms of "five, seven and a half, and ten," the author receives $700 a week if the play does $10,000 worth of business.

The author's royalties are always estimated on the *gross* receipts and are reckoned as an operating expense in the producer's cost-sheets.

Authors of prominence command higher royalty terms from the producers. Frequently, an author's royalties are scaled at 5% of the first $4,000 and then 7½% of the next $2,000 and 10% above. On such terms, the author's royalties are slightly higher than those cited previously.

As for instance, if a play is grossing $10,000 a week:

5% on the first $4,000	$200
7½% on the next $2,000	150
10% on the next $4,000	400
	$750 Total

Some important authors sometimes receive as high as a flat 10% of the gross. To command higher terms than the minimum, however, a playwright must enjoy great prestige and his manuscripts must be in demand.

In this matter, a shrewd agent is always of great value to the playwright. Since the agent earns 10% of the author's royalties for his services, naturally, he tries to get the best terms for the author he can drive with the producer.

HOW MUCH DOES A SUCCESSFUL PLAYWRIGHT EARN?

Answer: There is no doubt that playwriting can be the most lucrative form of writing for an author.

In the first place, once the play is out of the rehearsal stages and playing to an audience, the author's job is usually at an end, although the producer has a right to call on a playwright for revisions for three weeks after the opening of the play. In rare cases, an author will continue to make changes in a play for some time after the opening performance in the at-

So You Want to Be a Playwright? 53

tempt to improve the play for his own sake, as well as the producer's.

But certainly in the case of a play that opens successfully, the task of the playwright is at an end and he can sit back and enjoy his royalties.

Let us examine the hypothetical case of a play that is a "smash" hit and runs for a year on Broadway, and determine roughly what the author's earnings from such a success total:

1. For 20 weeks the show plays to capacity and grosses $18,000 a week. Each week the author receives (on a "five, seven and a half, and ten" basis) royalties of $1,500.

2. For the next 20 weeks the grosses average at $14,000 a week. Each week the author receives royalties of $1,100.

3. For the next 12 weeks, the grosses average $10,000 a week. Each week the author receives $750.

4. For the next 12 weeks, when the play is in the closing stages of its New York run, the grosses average $7,000 a week. Each week the author receives $400 a week.

5. The play may go on tour for 20 weeks and average grosses of $10,000 a week. Each week the author receives $750.

6. The play, being a "smash" hit, will probably have a motion picture sale of $60,000. The playwright's share (explained in a later passage) is $36,000.

7. The sale of publication rights, foreign rights, ama-

teur rights, radio rights, stock rights, etc., may bring the playwright an additional $75,000 on a "smash" hit play.

8. Perhaps an additional company may go on tour for approximately 20 weeks and average grosses of $10,000 a week. The author's share is $750 a week.

9. Year in, year out, the play may bring small sums to the author over a period of 10 or 15 years through occasional touring productions or foreign productions. Let us say arbitrarily that the total received from the playwright on his "smash" hit over a period of years totals to another $15,000.

Now for the total received by the playwright:

1. $30,000 (first 20 weeks in N. Y.)
2. 22,000 (second 20 weeks in N. Y.)
3. 9,000 (12 weeks in N. Y.)
4. 4,800 (final 12 weeks in N. Y.)
5. 15,000 (on tour)
6. 36,000 (motion picture rights)
7. 75,000 (additional rights)
8. 15,000 (second road company)
9. 15,000 (total future income)

$221,800 Total

Of course, "smash" hits can bring larger motion picture sales than $60,000. Also, more than one road company may be sent out, and royalties need not be the minimum of "five, seven and a half, and ten". In addition, the play may run for more than just one year

So You Want to Be a Playwright?

in New York. In such cases, the author's royalties swell. In the case of "Tobacco Road" and "Three Men on a Horse", for instance, the road companies are all doing enormous business and the Broadway engagements seem interminable.

But $221,800, less agent's commissions of 10%, is certainly a tidy sum. Perhaps not as great as what a Wall Street broker can earn on the Exchange, dabbling in a stock, but, all told, a very satisfactory mark to shoot for. Playwrights have earned such royalties and more from a single play.

These figures are calculated on the basis of a play being a "smash" hit. It may afford you some mental pleasure to speculate a bit with pencil and paper as to what a moderately successful play will bring an author in the way of royalties.

But, remember, in an entire Broadway season very rarely do more than a half a dozen "smash" hits turn up on the boards. And only about 30 plays a season enjoy any sort of an extended engagement. There are usually about 120 dramatic productions a season. Most of them are dismal "flops". A play that closes after one or two performances does not enrich the playwright, no matter how much work he may have put into writing his play.

Finally, if you do strike it rich, you will have to pay an increased income tax to the government!

DOES A SUCCESSFUL PLAYWRIGHT CONTINUE TO BE SUCCESSFUL?

Answer: That probably sounds a bit silly, but there is a real point behind the question.

The Broadway theatre is so constituted that the playwright is always on trial. Each time he has a play produced, he must pass the acid test of the "first night" performance. His reputation on the opening night will mean nothing if he does not "deliver". On Broadway a playwright's reputation is as good as his last play.

Even the most established authors have their failures, plays from which they may earn nothing above their advance royalties of a few hundred dollars. As a matter of fact, the demands on a successful playwright are increased because of his reputation. Each play must be better than the next, or at least as good, because things are expected of him.

Of course, such authors as Eugene O'Neill, George S. Kaufman, Marc Connelly, Robert E. Sherwood, Philip Barry, Elmer Rice, S. N. Behrman and others have written many successful plays, but examine the records of any of these men and you will discover that they have had their share of failures.

WHAT SHARE DOES THE PLAYWRIGHT RECEIVE OF A PICTURE SALE?

Answer: This question has acquired great importance in recent years, now that the moving picture industry, wired for sound, looks to the Broadway theatre for material.

Many plays are financed by motion picture companies eager to establish Broadway successes that can later be translated into the medium of the screen.

Many plays which are only moderately successful on Broadway are bought by the picture companies as potential screen material. As a result, producers have frequently produced plays in the expectation of a large picture sale, in many cases considering the picture rights more valuable than the chances for the play on Broadway.

Under the old Minimum Basic Agreement, the producer was required to present a play, with a first class production, for three consecutive weeks on Broadway or for 75 consecutive performances on tour. For this consideration, he received 50% of the picture rights, the author receiving the other 50%.

Convinced that many alliances between motion picture companies and producers have worked to the detriment of the author, the Dramatists' Guild recently created a new Minimum Basic Agreement, with a completely revised clause covering the disposition of motion picture rights. For one thing, it was felt by the Guild that a producer, financed by a motion picture company, could not represent an author fairly in the sale of the picture rights. For another thing, the premise that the sale of picture rights was on the open market for competitive bidding among the various picture companies seemed lacking in foundation to the members of the Dramatists' Guild, since it was apparent that a motion picture company that had "backed" the production of a play could limit the price of the sale. For, by owning a "piece of the show", the motion picture company had a share in the producer's 50% of the picture rights and, consequently, could always outbid another company and still acquire the picture rights at a price below what the other company was offering.

To correct this situation, the Dramatists' Guild created a new clause whereby the picture rights are the sole property of the author and are to be disposed of by a "negotiator" set up by the Dramatists' Guild. The old rule that a producer must present a play for three consecutive weeks on Broadway, or for 75 consecutive performances on tour, still holds good.

In exchange for this guaranteed engagement of a first class production, the producer now receives 40% of the money obtained from a motion picture sale. The balance of 60% goes to the author.

Thus, on a picture sale of $60,000, as already quoted in the hypothetical "smash" hit, the producer receives $24,000 and the playwright receives $36,000.

Under the former Minimum Basic Agreement, the producer and author shared equally, each receiving $30,000 on a picture sale of $60,000.

WHAT ARE THE OBLIGATIONS OF A PRODUCER TO A PLAYWRIGHT?

Answer: Boiled down, the answer is a first class production.

The author is consulted on casting, the choice of a director, and practically every item in the production of his play. On casting and the choice of a director, he has the final vote before either of these items may be completed. He is entitled and expected to attend all rehearsals of the play and to be present at the out-of town "try-out", if the play does not open "cold". His expenses incurred in attending such a "try-out" are defrayed by the producer.

In order to share in the rights to a play, as already explained, the producer must perform the play for three consecutive weeks in New York, or for 75 consecutive performances on tour. If he does not do so, all rights revert to the author. There have been many instances where a producer failed to meet this obligation and subsequently the play was bought by a picture company or produced abroad or on tour. In these cases, the playwright receives the entire revenue, despite the fact that the producer has invested money in producing the play.

The producer must pay to the author his royalties, which are due on the Saturday night of each week, within seven days after the end of each week. In addition, he must furnish the author with daily box-office statements, signed by the treasurer of the theatre in which the attraction is performed, within seven days after the end of each week. These statements must be countersigned by the producer or his authorized representative, usually the company-manager.

The producer must announce the name of the author on all programs and in any advertising matter where the name of the producer appears.

The producer usually sees to it that the playwright receives general newspaper publicity, although he is in no way bound to do this.

In short, an author who sells a play to a producer is an important and respected figure in the production of that play.

WHAT HAPPENS IF A DISPUTE ARISES BETWEEN PLAYWRIGHT AND PRODUCER?

Answer: In the event of any disagreement between the producer and playwright, the matter in dispute may be submitted to arbitration.

The complaint is first filed with the Dramatists' Guild and a copy of the complaint must be mailed to the party complained against by the aggrieved simultaneously. The party complained against must file an answer to the complaint with the Dramatists' Guild within seven days from the date of the mailing of the complaint.

The Guild appoints one arbitrator to represent the author and the producer also nominates one arbitrator to represent himself. These two arbitrators are appointed within seven days from the date of the mailing of the complaint.

The two arbitrators appoint a third arbitrator who is selected from a regular panel of 30 individuals. This panel is created jointly by the Dramatists' Guild and the producers who have signed the Minimum Basic Agreement. The third arbitrator must be chosen within ten days from the date of the mailing of the complaint.

If the two arbitrators fail to agree on a third arbitrator, the third arbitrator is selected by the Executive Secretary of The American Arbitration Association or by the Executive Secretary of the Association of the Bar of the City of New York from the previously mentioned panel of 30 individuals. (A substitute panel, selected by the Governor of the State of New York, is also provided.)

The arbitration hearing occurs not later than four days after the third arbitrator has been chosen and lasts for not more than three days, unless the arbitrators decide to extend the time of the hearing after a majority vote.

Neither playwright nor the producer is obligated to appear at the hearing, but the arbitrators may nevertheless proceed to hear and determine the case.

The decision of the arbitrators, after reviewing the complaint, is binding and final on both parties.

This all sounds like pretty grim stuff—but an author will do well to familiarize himself with the procedure, for quarrels between producers and authors, unfortunately, do occur. Most disputes, of course, can be settled amicably, and it is inadvisable for an author to be hot-headed and hold the club of arbitration over a producer's head. For one thing, the producer can win, particularly if he happens to be right!

In the case of a disagreement between an author and producer on the subject of the casting or rewriting of a play, the arbitration process is speeded up so that the arbitrators are selected within 48 hours after the filing of a complaint and a hearing held within 60 hours, since in such a dispute, the play is usually in production and a decision must be reached quickly.

Arbitration is a two-edged sword. It is designed to protect the author's brain-child from what he considers ruinous production and also to protect the producer, who has his production cost at stake, from a stubborn author.

WHAT IS THE "NEGOTIATOR"?

Answer: This is a new office, created by the Dramatists' Guild in connection with the latest Minimum Basic Agreement.

The "negotiator" is appointed by the Council of the Dramatists' Guild and ratified by a two-thirds

So You Want to Be a Playwright? 63

vote of all the producers who have signed the Minimum Basic Agreement. He acts as the representative of all member authors of the Dramatists' Guild in the transaction of the sale of motion picture rights of plays.

He supervises the drawing up of any contract between a motion picture company and an author on the sale of a play, receives all monies derived from the sale which are deposited in a special account of the Dramatists' Guild, and then makes payments to the author and the producer, if the latter is entitled to a share after fulfilling his contractual obligations to the author.

The Dramatists' Guild deducts $3\frac{1}{2}\%$ from the total picture sale of each play, deducted from agents' commissions, which is applied to a fund out of which the "negotiator" is paid for his services. (When the author acts as his own agent, the percentage is deducted from his share.) From this fund, the "negotiator" receives $3\frac{1}{2}\%$ of the gross annual picture sales transacted, but is limited to a maximum salary of $15,000 a year.

The "negotiator" may be removed by a two-thirds vote of the producers in good standing who have signed the Minimum Basic Agreement provided by the Dramatists' Guild, or by a two-thirds vote of the Council of the Guild.

The "negotiator" holds office indefinitely until he is removed or retires.

WHAT IS A "PLAY DOCTOR"?

Answer: This question is not too far a cry from the material that has immediately preceded.

A "play doctor" is frequently called in by a producer, after obtaining the author's written consent, to rewrite or revise a play that has defied the efforts of the original author.

As a result, a "play doctor" is your collaborator, and as such, will share in your royalties and your picture rights and is entitled to representation with you by the Dramatists' Guild and the "negotiator."

Sometimes this collaborator is brought in before the play is produced, if the producer is able to persuade the author that his play needs mending by an experienced hand before it can begin rehearsals.

Sometimes, the "play doctor" is called in after the play has gone into rehearsal and it becomes apparent that the play stands in need of revisions.

Again, there are occasions when a play goes out of town for its "try-out" performances and what seemed like a gloriously perfect venture in the theatre, on being shown to its first audience, proves to be more than slightly sour. The playwright will be quartered in a hotel room until he is so dizzy with fatigue and new developments of plot that he no longer has the

So You Want to Be a Playwright?

faintest notion of what he is banging out on his portable typewriter. Frantic conferences between playwright and producer and star and director usually ensue at this point. Next, hurried phone calls and telegrams to New York and enter the "play doctor."

There is a glorious legend told of no less a figure than George S. Kaufman who is reputed to have wired Sam Harris from New Haven while desperately at work revising a new play after its first "try-out" performance. The wire read, "Dear Sam everything fine but please send a second act typewriter immediately."

WHAT ARRANGEMENT DOES THE "PLAY DOCTOR" MAKE?

Answer: Almost invariably, he shares in the author's royalties. The amount that he receives depends on his reputation as an author and on how much work the play needs.

Here, again, an agent proves of service to the playwright by arranging the deal with the "play doctor".

A playwright usually surrenders between 25% and 50% of his royalties to the author who is called in to whip his play into shape. In some cases, the "play doctor" will also receive credit on the program as a co-author, particularly when he is well-known and his name is of value in the billing.

In rare cases, a "play doctor" will perform his services for a cash sum paid to him by the producer.

There are also instances where the producer himself may decide to do whatever rewriting is necessary in order to heighten the values of a play. Some producers will donate this service to the playwright, others will receive part of the author's royalties.

In any event, don't be surprised if you sell a play to a producer and discover that you need a collaborator. Unless you have extraordinary talent, your first play is not likely to be in shape for immediate production. Either you will be able to make the changes the producer asks for, or someone will be called in to do it for you; that is, if you want a production.

WHAT MAY HOLD UP PRODUCTION OF YOUR PLAY AFTER IT HAS BEEN BOUGHT?

Answer: Many things.

The fact that you have sold your play to a producer does not mean he is certain to produce it.

Frequently, producers buy several plays and then find there isn't enough time to do them all in one season.

Producers often buy plays and subsequently are unable to cast them satisfactorily and, as a result, abandon production plans.

Again, producers will find that they can't raise the money needed to produce the play, after having bought it.

There have even been rare cases when a producer will buy a play that he has no intention of producing himself, because he doesn't want a rival producer to acquire the play. This probably sounds absurd, but the theatre is a restricted little world and petty jealousies are rife among some producers.

Sometimes producers become enthusiastic about a play after first reading it and buy it immediately. But, on a second reading, they discover that the play is not as exciting as it seemed. This is what is known as going "cold" on a manuscript. Occasionally the producer goes "cold" because he discovers that the play will cost much more to produce than he had calculated before buying it.

There also are cases of a producer who has bought a play with the assurance that he has all his financing necessary for a production. A quarrel with the "backer" may leave him without that all-important financing, unable to raise it somewhere else, and the production will be abandoned.

Often a producer will buy a play because he thinks it has a good idea or situation. After exhaustive rewriting, he may discover that the play cannot be altered to his satisfaction, and release the play

A producer may buy a play, be fully prepared for production, and then receive a tempting offer to go to Hollywood for an executive position at a fabulous salary that he cannot resist. The playwright may get left at the post with his play unproduced, as a result.

There are also those occasions when a producer

buys a play in great excitement, sets the wheels into motion for production, and then gives the play to be read by some esteemed friend or person whose opinion he respects. That person may not like the play and proceed to talk the producer out of doing it. This is another version of going "cold". It is a rare one, fortunately for the playwright. Most producers trust their own judgment.

Illness, strikes, acts of God, are other factors that may forestall a production.

The new Minimum Basic Agreement protects the playwright considerably in that for $100 a producer acquires a play for one month and subsequently renews his options monthly. Formerly, the producer controlled the play for six months for an advance payment of anything up to $500. A producer who discovers, for one reason or another, shortly after buying a play, that he is not going to produce it, is not likely to renew his option and the playwright is free to take his manuscript to another producer for consideration. At least, a play is no longer tied up for six months.

WHAT ABOUT AMATEUR RIGHTS?

Answer: A new amateur play service has just been organized under the Dramatists' Guild for the use of members and associates. The director is Barrett H. Clark. The service will rent the plays of members and associates to non-professional theatres. Use of the service,

So You Want to Be a Playwright?

which will handle plays in the U. S. and also do a certain amount of publishing, is *optional,* and contracts will be uniform. Many authors realize a comfortable yearly income from the royalties obtained through amateur performances.

HOW IMPORTANT IS CASTING IN STARTING A PRODUCTION?

Answer: It is one of the most knotty problems that confronts a producer and playwright. Almost 50% of productions that are delayed are the result of casting problems.

Hollywood has made so many raids on Broadway talent in the ranks of the actors that it is extremely difficult to cast a play at will. A talented new young actor may crop up in a play, make a first night "hit", and promptly be snatched off by the picture scouts who "cover" all the openings.

One of the most bitter complaints made by the producers in recent years has been concerning the difficulty in casting a play well.

Often the one actor a producer may think most suited to play a certain role may be engaged in another production. In such a case, the producer may decide to sit back for a while until he is able to obtain that actor. This usually will mean sitting around and waiting for some other producer to have a "flop".

Frequently, producers make flying trips to Hollywood in the hope of inducing some celebrated screen player to return to the stage. In the last few seasons, there has been a growing tendency on the part of actors who have come from out of comparative obscurity in the theatre into silver-screen stardom to return to the theatre for an occasional stage appearance. But it is still a difficult business, for the theatre cannot afford to pay Hollywood salaries to actors nor can it guarantee weekly pay checks all year around. Again, most screen players are under long-term contract to their companies and find it difficult to get away from the movie lots for a long enough period of time in which to appear on Broadway in a play.

There are thousands of actors looking for work along Broadway, but very few of them have any reputation or sufficient experience for a producer to be willing to take a chance on them in leading roles.

SHOULD YOU WRITE A PLAY FOR A STAR?

Answer: There are two sides to this question.

If you write a play with a star in mind for the leading role, you are putting all your eggs in one basket.

Through devious means, you may get the star to read the play you have labored over and discover that he or she doesn't happen to like your play.

Also, stars sometimes lay their plans far ahead. So that they may even admire your play and still be unable to say when they will be able to rehearse in it, no matter how important a producer sends it to them.

Finally, there are very few stars who command a

So You Want to Be a Playwright?

real box-office following. Having a star appear in your play is not a positive guarantee of fame and fortune, unless you happen to have landed one of the few whose name on the theatre marquee still insures a definite audience. Katharine Cornell, Leslie Howard, Alfred Lunt and Lynn Fontanne, George M. Cohan, Ina Claire, Elizabeth Bergner, Jane Cowl, Noel Coward, Gertrude Lawrence, and a very few others, command a "following". And even they cannot carry for very long a play that has been attacked by the critics.

Your best bet is to write a play because you think it's good, not just because you have thought of a stunning leading role for a star. If you can write a good play that can use a star, fine and dandy.

On the other hand, if you can write a good play that simply requires a competent cast, you are even better off. You will save a producer a lot of trouble and your play is more likely to be produced quickly.

Only too often producers are heard wailing. "The play is great but I need a *terrific* actor to play the lead and I can't find anybody!"

WHAT DOES IT COST TO PRODUCE A PLAY?
Answer: Turn to the section of this book devoted to producers and read it carefully.

Every playwright should have some knowledge of what it costs a producer to do a show. It will be of real assistance in the plotting of a play. If you can possibly spare the producer expense when writing a play, you should do so, providing you do not harm your play. That is, a playwright should not lean over backward to write a play that requires only one set of scenery. If you can do it, without cramping the action of your play, splendid, but if your play needs a change of locale to heighten the action, by all means write your play that way.

You needn't be worried because you have written a play that will be expensive to produce, for if it is a really good play, its production cost will not frighten a producer off. The point is that a good play should be written economically, both for artistry and for practical reasons.

WHAT IS A RENEWAL CLAUSE?

Answer: The clause in the author's contract with the producer which gives the producer the right to renew his option on the play monthly for one year.

If the producer does not exercise this option, by making monthly payments of advance royalties, the play reverts to the author.

At the end of one year, if the producer has not yet produced the play, he no longer has the option to renew. To retain the play, he must draw up a new contract with the author and all previous advance payments of royalties are lost by the producer.

WHY DOES A PLAY GO ON THE ROAD BEFORE A NEW YORK PREMIÈRE?

Answer: There was a time when practically every play

So You Want to Be a Playwright?

was given an out-of-town "try-out" before coming to New York. This is known as "trying it on the dog".

The reasons for such a test are fairly obvious, to get an audience reaction to the performance and to make whatever revisions in the manuscript and cast seem necessary.

Comedies, particularly, require playing before an audience in order to determine where the big laughs are and to "time" the show. It's one of the theatre's major peculiarities that practically no one can be positive about a play by just watching it in rehearsal. Scenes that may seem to be packed with drama sometimes become absurd when played before an audience. The crowd psychology in a theatre often upsets the best-laid plans of a playwright, producer, director, and cast.

However, there has been a growing tendency in the professional theatre to eliminate preliminary road tours for a play. For one thing, such engagements are often costly to the producer, since audiences out of New York do not always come to see a play that is not already a proven New York success, unless there is a star in the play or some other attraction connected with it. Also, out-of-town audiences are not always a positive test. There have been many instances where plays that seemed like sure-fire successes on the road came into New York and were failures. Reversely, plays that limped along on the road have become great successes in New York.

The point is that the New York first-night audience is an extremely peculiar assemblage and there is no real gauging of what it will like or dislike after that breathless moment when the curtain rises.

As a result, many producers now open their plays "cold". That is, they do not take the play out of town for a preliminary engagement. Instead they give invitation dress rehearsals prior to the official première. Sometimes, these dress rehearsal audiences are benefit performances where the tickets are sold to organizations and societies. It has even become slightly fashionable for an organization to "buy out" a preview performance of a new play.

There have been several instances where, after a series of dress rehearsals before invited or paid audiences, the producer has decided not to open the play until revisions have been made, or even to abandon the production entirely. This is very much the same procedure that is followed when going out of town for a "try-out".

The playwright, however, is better off when the producer decides to "try it on the dog." If the play seems wobbly and in need of rewriting, the producer can always book another week in another city, allowing the playwright more time to get the play in shape for the Broadway opening. It also gives the cast a

So You Want to Be a Playwright?

chance to become at home in the play and to try new pieces of "business" on an audience.

WHAT ARE THE ADVANTAGES OF A SUMMER "TRY-OUT"?

Answer: There are also two sides to this question, although the majority opinion would seem to be that a summer "try-out" is extremely risky for a playwright.

Each summer, in dozens of barns, community centers, and what not, up and down the Atlantic seaboard, there are companies of professional actors who give performances of plays. Mostly, the plays are revivals of established Broadway successes. But there are also frequent performances of new plays, done prior to Broadway, in the hope of discovering some potential gold mine.

Only a limited few of these summer theatres are well enough equipped with adequate production facilities and good actors for a playwright to be able to judge very much about his play. Usually, the best thing that can be determined about a play through a summer theatre production is that it is bad. This, of course, is of value to an author; for if he can determine that his play is not worth bothering about any further, he can save himself a great deal of time and energy.

Most plays, performed in summer theatres, receive only a week of rehearsal, at the most two weeks. This is hardly sufficient time for a company of actors and a director to do a finished creative job on a new play. Again, it is a rare summer theatre that can provide an author with a really good cast. It is usually a makeshift performance and the result is that the playwright is totally at sea about his play.

Thus far, very few plays given preliminary performances in a summer theatre have subsequently become even moderate successes in New York.

There are some summer theatres which manage to enlist excellent resident companies and can attract important guest stars. But, even in this group, extremely few are able to execute finished physical productions. Scenery and lighting is seldom of the best and many make-shift devices are used as emergency measures.

Of the summer theatres that are more or less established as first-rate there are Stockbridge, Westport, Southampton, Dennis, Mount Kisco, Newport, Skowhegan, Locust Valley, Falmouth, and Ivorytown. Prominent Broadway producers have tested new plays at these theatres and, occasionally, plays have been brought to Broadway the following fall as a result of such engagements.

Most agents are reluctant to entrust a promising manuscript to the exigencies of a summer theatre performance. The truth of the matter is that a playwright has very little to gain from such a production and a great deal to lose.

However, the summer theatres are valuable for

So You Want to Be a Playwright?

laboratory experience. A playwright who is learning how to write plays can do worse than get a summer theatre production. At least, he is able to watch the entire operation of a production and to profit from seeing his play performed before an audience. As such, the summer theatres are valuable to a playwright.

ARE THERE ANY EXPERIMENTAL THEATRES IN NEW YORK?

Answer: The sad truth of the matter is that production in the New York theatre is almost entirely restricted to Broadway.

The halcyon days in the New York theatre which saw the development of such rebel groups as the Provincetown Players, the old Washington Square Players, and the Theatre Guild are memories. No organized experimental groups have come along to replace them. As a result there is small opportunity for an author to experiment in New York.

The Theatre Guild has become one of the most puissant members in the ranks of the Broadway producers and is essentially a commercial institution. The Group Theatre gives its productions in the Broadway sector and is faced with typically high production costs which strangle daring experiment. The Theatre Union, an insurgent organization of the Left, operates off Broadway in the old Civic Repertory Theatre on 14th Street. These three organizations will be discussed shortly under separate headings.

In the main, a playwright must write for Broadway if he is seeking New York production and attention. He has practically no opportunity to learn how to write plays, except through repeated Broadway productions. There are no little "art" groups, operated by competent people with a passion for the theatre, to whom he can turn for production in New York.

The only recent new movement in the theatre to be found off Broadway is to be discovered among a number of labor groups and organizations who are interested expressly in social and political drama. These organizations are badly handicapped for production facilities and by a lack of funds. The Theatre of Action and The Theatre Collective are two organizations typical of this movement and derive their inspiration from the more successful efforts of the Theatre Union.

In order to write for such groups, one must have positive political sentiments, leaning strongly to the Left, and express them rigidly in the theatre. So far, at least, such plays must follow a working-class point of view so that the playwright is limited ideologically.

These organizations are better equipped to produce short plays although some major productions have been given.

The audiences for the theatre of the Left are frequently exciting and highly responsive emotionally, sometimes to the point where they lean over backward

So You Want to Be a Playwright?

in enthusiasm for a play that is far from a polished effort. However, the theatre of the Left is young and growing and its audiences are learning rapidly to make increased demands on the playwright. It is the only field in the New York theatre that affords a playwright the opportunity for genuine experiment.

But the old free "art" theatre, the kind patterned after Antoine and the Théâtre Libre, is not to be found in New York today. If you are a playwright, without political convictions, and are seeking New York production, you will have to write for Broadway.

For experiment, off Broadway, you can turn to the summer theatres or else to a very limited group of university theatres which function throughout the nation.

HOW DOES THE THEATRE GUILD BUY PLAYS?

Answer: The Theatre Guild is the sole remaining "hang-over" from the days in the New York theatre when the experimental theatre flourished. It has become rich and powerful and is easily the most important producing force in the American theatre.

It has a guaranteed subscription audience which assures the return of most production costs. It is founded on the principle of producing "good" plays, but sometimes strays into rather restricted commercial fields.

The Theatre Guild is guided by a board of directors who have controlled its destinies ever since it was first organized in 1919. Year in, year out, the Theatre Guild has produced a minimum of 6 plays a year. No major decisions are made by the Theatre Guild board except through a unanimous vote, a principle adopted and followed from its very inception.

With a constant obligation to its subscribers, the strain of producing that is imposed on the directors of the Theatre Guild is unquestionably severe.

As a result, selling a play to the Theatre Guild is far from easy. Getting a production from the Theatre Guild, after having sold the organization a play, is even more uncertain. The Theatre Guild is more or less obligated in longer or shorter periods to produce the works of several distinguished authors, Eugene O'Neill, Behrman, and Maxwell Anderson, to name a few. As a result, the chances for a new author to receive a Theatre Guild production are slim. However, the chance does exist. The Theatre Guild is still able and willing to make experiments. George O'Neil, Lynn Riggs, and John Wexley, among others, have received productions by the Theatre Guild through having written unusual plays.

Certainly a Theatre Guild production is one to be prized, for the Guild has the best in everything to bring to the production of a play. Furthermore, the prestige of a Theatre Guild production is worth its weight in gold to a playwright. Even if an author sells a play to the Theatre Guild and is not fortunate enough to have it produced it is valuable to him, for the play is immediately enhanced in the eyes of the Broadway producers.

Incidentally, make no mistake about it, the Broadway producers are interested in producing good plays. Many of them have fine taste, a literate approach to the theatre, and distinct integrity. It also is axiomatic along Broadway that a good play will almost always make money.

HOW DOES THE GROUP THEATRE BUY PLAYS?

Answer: While the Group Theatre functions in the Broadway district, its members are interested in plays that have social implications. It is the attitude of this organization that a play need not be obvious Left propaganda to have social content, a distinction that is sometimes fine and more than a little confusing. Boiled down, the Group Theatre theory is that any play that causes an audience to think in terms of organized society is of value. The thought content may come out of comedy, or it may come out of drama.

The Group has produced such plays as "The House of Connelly", a play about a decadent aristocratic Southern family; "Men in White", describing internal conditions in a metropolitan hospital; "Success Story", a play about an egoist in the advertising business; "Awake and Sing", a play about a bourgeois New York Jewish family, etc.

The Group is headed by a board of directors, Harold Clurman, Cheryl Crawford and Lee Strasberg, whose decisions are sometimes ratified by the members of the acting company. Harold Clurman is the managing director of the organization.

Before a play is accepted for production by the Group, it must first win the approval of the three directors as suitable to the Group method of acting. Since the Group is composed of a permanent acting company, it is highly important that the roles in the play are such as lend themselves to performance by the company. But, since the company is a well-rounded one, this is not always a limitation.

The Group produces plays under the same conditions that any commercial Broadway producer does, and pays an author the regular royalties and advances. Clifford Odets, considered by many critics the most promising young playwright in the American theatre, emerged as a playwright out of the Group's own acting company.

The Group obtains its financing through the regular commercial methods, from motion picture companies, "angels", etc. However, it always attempts to create a sinking fund out of profits for the purpose of supporting the company all year around and for future productions. Frequently the entire company goes off into the country for the summer to rehearse a new play over an extended period of time.

HOW DOES THE THEATRE UNION BUY PLAYS?

Answer: The Theatre Union, too, is conducted by a board of directors, consisting of about a dozen people. Before the Theatre Union buys a play and produces it, there must be practically a unanimous vote among the directors of the organization.

Among the directors of the Theatre Union are a number of playwrights, including Albert Maltz, George Sklar, Paul Peters, Victor Wolfson and Michael Blankfort, all of whom have written plays that have been produced by the Union.

In buying a play, the Union signs the same author's contract as is signed by any Broadway producer. But, since the Theatre Union presents its plays at reduced prices, the gross receipts are never very much over $6,000 a week, so that the maximum royalties a playwright may earn through a Theatre Union production cannot be over a few hundred dollars a week.

However, the Theatre Union employs a very successful method of obtaining audiences through organized theatre parties, whereby the Theatre Union is guaranteed either sold-out houses or the sale of blocks of seats. In addition, the operating costs of the Theatre Union are scaled low. There are no stars in Theatre Union casts and no high salaries. As a result, the Theatre Union is able to keep a play running over an extended period of time, even in the face of an indifferent critical reception.

The Theatre Union is a non-profit organization and none of its directors draw salaries, unless they perform a specific job on a production throughout its run, such as stage-managing, or handling publicity, etc.

The Theatre Union obtains its financing through every possible channel, loans, drives for funds, gifts, production fund taxes, dances, dinners, etc.

The Theatre Union is definitely of the Left politically, with a labor class point of view. Thus far, it has produced such plays as "Peace on Earth", an anti-war play; "Stevedore", a play concerned with the problems of the Negro race; "Sailors of Cattaro", a play describing a mutiny in the Austrian fleet during the World War; "Bitter Stream", an anti-Fascist play, etc. The platform of the Theatre Union is broad and embraces many social subjects.

One item in the Theatre Union method, of interest to playwrights, is the fact that a committee, composed of playwright members of the Theatre Union Board, devotes itself to consulting with authors whose plays seem promising for purposes of Theatre Union production. This committee suggests revisions in a play that will make a manuscript acceptable to the Theatre Union.

So You Want to Be a Playwright?

DOES A PLAYWRIGHT MAKE MORE MONEY THAN A PRODUCER OUT OF A SUCCESSFUL PLAY?

Answer: In most cases the producer makes the big money out of a success, particularly if the play is a "smash" and if his operating costs are low.

Whereas a playwright may earn royalties of $1,500 a week on a successful play, a producer may net a weekly profit of several times that amount. In the case of "Tobacco Road", for instance, while the authors of that play are earning large royalties, the producers are netting profits that are enormous. "Tobacco Road" is a one-set play, with a small cast, requiring only one high-salaried actor. The production cost was ridiculously cheap and the play can break even at gross receipts of $3,000 a week. The Broadway production and two road companies are all playing to huge business. The total weekly profit for the producers is staggering, running between $3,000 and $8,000 a week.

Similarly in the case of "Dead End", the producer's weekly profits are much higher than the royalties received by the author.

However, in both the productions of "Tobacco Road" and "Dead End", the authors, Jack Kirkland and Sidney Kingsley, respectively, are partners in the producer's profits, having invested money in the productions. As a result, they share not only in the royalties but in the other profits, as well.

HOW MANY PLAYWRIGHTS ARE PRODUCERS?

Answer: Comparatively few playwrights function openly as producers, although Elmer Rice made a fortune not only out of writing "Counsellor-at-Law", but by directing and producing it as well.

Some producers have an occasional fling at playwriting, as for example, Arthur Hopkins, Lawrence Langner and John Golden.

Usually, a playwright who is interested in earning money as a producer out of his own plays invests money in a production and acts as a silent partner with some established producer. Producing plays is a full-time business and most playwrights are too busy writing plays to head a producing organization. Philip Barry, for instance, has invested his own money in plays of his which have been produced by Arthur Hopkins. Noel Coward has financed partially several of his plays produced by Max Gordon and recently formed a producing firm with Alfred Lunt and Lynne Fontanne, which is represented by John C. Wilson.

SHOULD A PLAYWRIGHT DIRECT HIS OWN PLAY?

Answer: This is a moot point. Playwrights have frequently directed their own plays, but often with indifferent results.

The fact that a playwright knows the content of his play thoroughly does not necessarily mean that he can direct it thoroughly. Directing is a specialized job and while a director should know something about playwriting, it does not follow that a playwright is a competent director.

On the contrary, a playwright may be so "close" to his play, that he may over-direct it and dwell upon points in it that have special intellectual significance to him but which may bore an audience if scored too heavily in the direction.

There are playwrights who happen to be skilled directors. But even in such cases, a playwright who happens to be an able director is likely to do a better job of directing on someone else's play than his own, though there are specific exceptions to such a rule, viz., George S. Kaufman and Sidney Kingsley.

A playwright can help a director by sitting behind him during rehearsals and observing the growth of the play in performance. Frequently a director may bring things to a play that the author did not realize were important while writing the play. Again, a director can often suggest changes that may improve the play because he has a complete picture of how the play should seem to an audience.

It's best to have someone else direct your play, unless you are positive you have talent as a director and can do a good job on your own show.

Finally, since many producers are directors in their own right and produce plays because they want to direct them, the entire problem may be taken out of your hands.

WHY DO PLAYWRIGHTS GO TO HOLLYWOOD?

Answer: To make money.

The motion picture companies are confronted with the problem of fulfilling huge production schedules each year. They are constantly in search of new authors who can write successful scenarios, either original or adapted.

As soon as a playwright has a Broadway success, Hollywood usually makes flattering offers to him. Motion picture salaries for authors are dazzling, particularly to a new young author who has not yet experienced the taste of earning big money. Salaries begin at such figures as $400 a week and scale up to such sums as $1,500 or $2,500 a week. Often, when a playwright refuses the first offer made to him by a picture company, the offers of salary increase until the playwright is practically unable to refuse.

But playwrights who go to Hollywood and stay there for long on the fat of the land, stop being playwrights. The exceptions are rare.

SECTION III

SO YOU WANT TO BE A PRODUCER?

"I think that a person must have phenomenal dynamics to be able successfully to start his career as master of the economic, literary and artistic conditions of a theatre. If an experienced person is entrusted with, or owns, the money which operates the theatre, he is liable to make blunders in all departments, unless he has as consultants matured and mellowed theatrical people. I should think that it is best to master one or, at most, two phases of the complicated and delicate machinery of the theatre at one time. Reducing the theatre to its L.C.D. I have sometimes compared it with a man who has a flair for running a Punch and Judy show. He builds his show box, makes, paints and dresses his puppets, writes his story and then goes out on the street, sets up his box, works his puppets, characterizing them by change of voice, and, when he has aroused his audience to a pitch of enthusiasm, dashes out of his box to pass the hat. This would imply expert ability as a carpenter, an artist, a dressmaker, an elocutionist, an author, plus personality and magnetism. If a man has all these innately, then surely the best way for him to start in the theatre is as a producer."

— HARRY WAGSTAFF GRIBBLE, *successful freelance director, in a letter to the author*

SO YOU WANT TO BE A PRODUCER?

Answer: Being a producer would seem to be the most pleasant position one can hold in the theatre if you are a success.

Once the rehearsal period is over and the play is launched, the first-night hysteria in limbo, and excerpts from the "rave" notices inserted in the morning-after papers, the task of the producer is comparatively at an end and he can go off on an extended holiday if the mood seizes him. The white sands of Florida or Bermuda beckon invitingly to the producer whose show in New York town is bringing in handsome grosses and profits each week. His profits are usually larger than those of anyone connected with his successful attraction, including those of the author or star of the piece.

He is constantly sought out by actors, playwrights, agents, directors, technicians. He is the entrepreneur, the man of judgment, the source of activity in the theatre. His private office is an inner sanctum and an audience with him is eminently desirable. His telephone and private cable brings him in contact with people in London and Hollywood. His hours are his own and he can come to work at any hour he pleases, or not at all. He makes annual trips to Europe. He maintains a handsome apartment and country house, orders a special brand of cigarette and the best Scotch for his bar. His opening nights are aglitter with Society and Celebrities.

He is a kind of potentate.

He is also a human being.

There you have a nice rosy picture of the producer sitting on top of the theatre heap. It all spells success, luxury, power. It's an enviable position.

Very few producers know what it's like.

HOW DO YOU BECOME A PRODUCER?

Answer: It's very simple.

All you have to do is get or have "backing" and you can become a producer.

Anyone with money and a mind to do it is free to take an office and put his name on the door as a producer. The theatre is a green pasture and anyone with financing can wander into it. There is no committee that passes judgment on you and says whether or not you have sufficient ability or experience to qualify. You can be a venerable greybeard or you can be a raw blade out of college. You can be a man or a woman. You need never have seen a play on a stage. In fact, you don't have to know anything about the theatre. If you have a bank-roll — and it doesn't matter where you get it from — you can be a producer, for better or worse.

But if you start out as a producer and don't know

So You Want to Be a Producer?

your job thoroughly, the chances are you'll lose every cent you have and that will be the end of that — unless you can raise more money and do another show.

Anyone with backing can become a producer, but remaining a producer is a horse of a different hue. Producing a play is a very tricky business; the accent is on business. . . .

WHAT DOES A PRODUCER DO?

Answer: As already indicated, his most important task is to put up or raise the money needed to produce the show. That's the hard-boiled answer, the one you're likely to get from the boys along Broadway, and the practical one.

However, there are other functions which the producer may assume, varying according to the latitude of his talents and interests, which may be maximum or minimum.

Gordon Craig once insisted that the only man suited to hold the position of producer in the theatre is a designer. Craig's point is open to dispute, but certainly a thorough producer should know at least the basic elements of designing. There are any number of producers who, when presented with a blue print of a set, do not have the slightest notion as to the content and meaning of that print and, consequently, can offer very little by way of suggestion or criticism to a designer. Since a producer must foot the bills for building the scenery, he should know something about what he is paying for, before that blue print becomes actual scenery!

Before proceeding any further along this tack, it should be established once again, however, that a producer need possess none of this technical knowledge, since he can always hire people who do. But, for the purposes of this text, it might be more salutary to seek the well-rounded producer.

There are a host of producers who direct their productions. This predicates for the producer an intimate association with the play from the time of first reading the manuscript until the opening night of the production. From the point of view of artistry in the commercial theatre, the producer who directs is an all-round man, not just a figure-head. In addition, he saves the cost of engaging a director.

The producer, particularly when he also assumes the office of director, is responsible for the casting of a play, allowing the author a final veto on any decision. This means the producer must be familiar with the acting talent on Broadway. It requires his attending many plays to see performances, keeping casting files, interviewing new people, familiarizing himself constantly with as many actors as possible.

One of the prime duties that faces a producer is to estimate the production and operating budgets of a production. In short, he must determine how much it will cost to "ring up the curtain" on a play — that is, all the costs until the opening night — and how much it will cost to operate the play each week after it opens.

This means being a business-man, figuring where one can cut costs and where it is wise to be extravagant.

Sometimes by being extravagant, a producer wins the reputation of being a "showman." That is, you raise a great hullabaloo, spend money like water, in order to bring money in at the box-office.

In this connection, a shrewd producer is also an expert publicity man. He will devise methods of exploiting his production through advertising in the press, by using vivid posters throughout the country, by engaging people to enlist theatre parties among clubs and organizations, etc. It will sometimes entail exploiting certain elements in a play. Viz., a play about birth control will have an appeal in the producer's mind for certain organizations. He will direct the publicity on his play to interest such an audience if he thinks that will bring business, or avoid it like the plague if he thinks that will hurt the general business for the play.

It is apparent that a producer may be, and sometimes is, a scene designer, business manager, promoter, director, casting expert, publicity man and sociologist, all rolled into one. It is to his advantage to know something about all of these aspects of the theatre, but it isn't necessary entirely, since a crackerjack staff can relieve the producer of any or all of these responsibilities.

So far this is general, but it indicates how complex the job of a producer can be. Now to be more specific:
HOW DOES A PRODUCER GET STARTED?
Answer: Let us assume that he already has all the backing he needs to produce a play, or at least part of it.

With this established, his next step is to find a manuscript worthy of production in his opinion.
HOW DOES A PRODUCER FIND A PLAY?
Answer: He reads and reads and reads. Manuscript after manuscript, until his eyes are weary, his courage dashed, and his nerves on edge.

He may have an assistant to help him read, but unless he has absolute confidence in the reader he will be reluctant to entrust this job to anyone since he will never know when a "gold mine" has been passed up by the reader. The best he can hope from the reader is that he sort out the potential wheat from the obvious chaff.

There are two methods of obtaining manuscripts. They come either from the playbrokers who represent authors or direct from the authors themselves.

Sometimes a producer may have a play or the idea for a play described to him by an author over the luncheon table. Sometimes a producer may decide that a book or story he has read or heard about will make

So You Want to Be a Producer?

a good play. In the latter case he may commission an author to adapt the play for him after he has purchased or obtained the dramatic rights to the book or story.

There are also foreign plays which a producer may buy after having seen a performance abroad or after having read the manuscript in literal translation. Here again the question of adaptation frequently is involved.

The problem is to scour every available source for manuscripts and to read them all in the hope of finding a play that seems worth producing.

WHAT IS A PLAY "WORTH" PRODUCING?

Answer: One of two things:

Either it seems like a play that will make money or else it seems as though it will bring the producer prestige and honor even though it may lose money.

A producer is at all times interested in making money. But sometimes, particularly if he is a newcomer, he has small prestige as a producer and, as a result, does not receive in his office what are potentially the most commercial manuscripts for his consideration. In such a case, he is frequently wise to produce a play that he believes will bring him artistic kudos and a reputation.

In this connection, the revival of an accepted classic is sometimes "worth" producing, because it will give the producer an opportunity to reveal his taste and ability as a producer on a play that is a known quantity.

With the raids that Hollywood has made on the ranks of the Broadway playwrights, the established agents find that they have very few good manuscripts to send to the producers. As a result, when they do receive a good manuscript from an author they are inclined to send that manuscript to a producer in whom they have confidence.

Consequently, a new producer has to establish himself before he can hope to interest the better agents and authors. The best way of winning their admiration is to produce a play that makes money. Broadway always admires financial success. A "smash" hit will establish any producer. But often a *"succès d'estime"* is valuable to a producer. That is, a play that receives excellent reviews for its merit as a play and its style in production, even though it does not enjoy a long engagement.

WHAT HAPPENS AFTER A PRODUCER HAS READ A PLAY HE LIKES?

Answer: He buys the play.

This is accomplished by paying to the author or to the author's agent an advance in royalties on signing the standard contract provided by the Dramatists' Guild. Until recently, the producer was required to pay an advance of $500 to acquire a play. For this sum he was entitled to own the play for 6 months,

So You Want to Be a Producer?

with the option of renewing his rights for an additional 6 months by paying another $500 advance.

A new ruling of the Dramatists' Guild permits the producer to pay $100 to own the play for a month and an additional $100 each month for the next 5 months. After the first 6 months have elapsed, the producer may renew his option by paying $150 a month. If he has not produced the play at the end of one year, all rights revert to the author.

During the period that the producer owns the play, he proceeds to raise the rest of his backing, if he is short of what he thinks it will take to do the play. He will also set about casting and arranging the entire production of the play.

Some producers take their time about producing a play.

Some producers rush into production immediately.

The option period is frequently used by the producer for revising the play, either by the author, or by a "play-doctor".

We are now at the stage in the production of a play when the producer, after exhaustive reading of manuscripts, has finally found a play he is willing to produce.

It should be scored again that this is the basis of all production in the Broadway theatre. The play *is* the thing. It is more important than superb scenery, expert lighting, extravagant costumes, etc. Very rarely can a great star "carry" an inferior manuscript. Without the manuscript, the producer cannot begin to produce.

All right, then, we are at the point where the producer has found a manuscript that has won his enthusiasm. He is willing to gamble his money, his time, his talent, his energy, because he thinks he will have a success, of one kind or another.

WHAT DOES IT COST TO PRODUCE A PLAY?
Answer: This is a good point at which to take a deep breath.

There are many factors that enter into estimating the cost of a production.

Production costs of plays vary radically. But for a producer to be well equipped to produce even an inexpensive play, he should have at least $10,000 on hand to meet his immediate costs and for subsequent carrying costs.

However, plays have been produced for considerably less and more than that sum. For example, a play called "Precedent", a production that required many sets and a large cast, was produced at the Provincetown Theatre for approximately $1,000 and subsequently was moved to Broadway where it enjoyed a dignified run of many months.

But another play, produced by one of the managers of "Precedent", demanding only one set of scenery and a small cast, cost over $19,000, and yet had a brief

So You Want to Be a Producer? 101

engagement even though it was performed with a celebrated star heading the cast.

Now, bear in mind that $19,000 is far from an extravagant capitalization in producing a play. Many plays cost $50,000 and more to produce. "Grand Hotel", "The Good Earth", "Dinner at Eight", "She Loves Me Not", "Merrily We Roll Along", "Victoria Regina" and scores of other plays, all took a pretty penny to produce. Some have been successes and made money. Others have proven dismal failures.

Frequently expensive productions run for a long time and still do not make any money.

In this connection, the factor of the operating cost of a play is just as important as that of the production cost. This can be explained in very simple terms.

Let us say that a play costs $50,000 to produce. On the other hand, it may also cost $8,000 a week to operate. This operating cost includes salaries for actors; staff salaries; advertising and printing; royalties; office expenses; rentals of costumes, electrical equipment, properties, and furniture; stage-hands, etc.

(The normal staff a producer engages for a production includes a press agent, a stage manager, a company manager, a secretary, and perhaps a general manager.)

Let us now say that this $50,000 production has been favorably received by the press and proceeds to take in at the box-office $14,000 a week. At first glance it would appear that the weekly net profit is $6,000, deducting an $8,000 operating cost from a $14,000 gross. But there is also the factor of the theatre rental to be considered. Since the rental is usually calculated on a percentage of the weekly gross whereby the manager may only receive 60% of the gross receipts, the net gross for the producer on $14,000 will be only approximately $8,400. Thus, his actual net profit on the week is only $400. At the rate of $400 a week, it will take a very long time for the producer to get back his $50,000, even though the play continues to run to large audiences!

The operating cost here is too high. In order to make any money the producer must get bigger and better grosses, or else reduce his overhead.

(In addition, weekly grosses sometimes fall for one reason or another. Take such simple examples as inclement weather or Lent. They have a direct effect on theatre business.)

Of course, this is an extreme case, but parallel situations have occurred regularly in the commercial theatre.

There are other sources of profit on a play, however, which sometimes help a producer realize his investment and even net a profit. There are road companies, foreign rights, publication rights, stock rights, and, most important in this connection, his share of the motion picture rights.

So You Want to Be a Producer?

HOW IS A PRODUCTION BUDGETED?

Answer: There are various approaches to this question. But, boiled down, it all depends on how the producer feels that the play should be done. If he thinks it needs a star and a glittering cast, expensive costumes, scenery, etc., in order to win a public, the costs go up. If he thinks he has a "sure-fire" script that merely requires a competent cast and production, his costs are reduced.

At this point, it is worth while to note that in recent Broadway seasons, some of the biggest money-makers have been plays that were done without "names" in the cast or extravagant productions. For example, "The Children's Hour", "Tobacco Road", "Personal Appearance", "Boy Meets Girl", "Three Men on a Horse" and "Dead End" are all plays without stars and yet all proved great "hits".

But, by the same token, "Victoria Regina", "Jumbo", and "Pride and Prejudice" were based on glittering productions to attract and satisfy the public.

On page 104 is the production budget, detail by detail, as planned by a producer for a play that eventually proved to be a failure. It was on these figures that the producer estimated the potential cost of his production. It was a one-set play and required only eight actors. But he felt the play needed a star and a brilliant supporting cast in order for it to be a success.

Equity Bond	$5,200	(covering 2 weeks' cast salaries)
Scenery	2,800	(building and painting only)
Designer's fee	500	
Advance Royalty	500	
Costumes	1,000	
Furniture	300	(2 weeks rental)
Properties	250	(outright purchase)
Electrical Equipment	250	(2 weeks' rental)
Dress Rehearsals	600	(stage-hands' salaries)
Hanging scenery	150	(" " ")
Hauling	150	
Crew	250	(1 week of rehearsal)
Technician	400	(4 weeks of supervision)
Press Agent	150	(2 weeks)
Business Manager	400	(4 weeks)
Director	1,500	
Stage Manager	200	(4 weeks)
Secretary	100	(4 weeks)
Auditor	50	
Legal fees	250	
Insurance	150	
Photographs	150	
Frames	75	
Printing	150	
Office Expenses	250	
Transportation	100	
Bond for stage-hands	660	
Advance advertising	500	
Houseboards	100	
Typing parts	25	
Incidentals	250	
Reserve fund	2,500	
	$19,810	Total Production Cost

In this case, the producer knew that his star would be a sufficient inducement for a theatre owner to sign a straight percentage contract on a theatre. Otherwise

So You Want to Be a Producer?

the producer might have had to count on posting a cash guarantee of the theatre's expenses for one week, which would have run as follows:

Manager	$ 150.00
Treasurer	75.00
Asst. "	54.00
Doorman	16.00
Porter	20.00
Gallery Doorman	15.00
Head Usher	16.00
Ushers (8)	76.80
Maids (2)	12.00
Cleaners (5)	57.00
Engineer	55.50
Fireman	48.75
Stage Doorman	20.00
Night Watchman	21.00
Superintendent	25.00
Light and Heat	200.00
Incidentals	150.00
Advertising	250.00
Stage Crew (4)	279.00

$1,541.05 Total Theatre Expenses

Fortunately, in the case of this production, no theatre guarantee was required. But the producer was able to estimate that he needed $20,000 in order to produce the play at all well. This was the amount of money he raised.

The play went out of town for a week and then came into New York after the try-out. The reviews were luke warm and the play ran for several weeks to moderate business. Practically the entire investment was lost.

It took weeks and weeks of planning and negotiating until the cast was engaged and all arrangements for the production completed. It took four additional weeks of rehearsal and a week of playing out of town. The play ran for three weeks. The producer didn't make a cent. His backers lost over $15,000.

HOW IS A "SHOE-STRING" PRODUCTION BUDGETED?

Answer: The production of "Precedent", already referred to, was the lowliest kind of a "shoe-string" venture. It proved to be that rare miracle in the theatre, a play which was produced for "coffee and cakes" and yet became a success.

Before examining the figures involved, a few colorful facts about the production are in good order.

The play was produced by three energetic young men who had never before produced a play. They were sublimely ignorant of the task they had set for themselves and, as a result, could not be discouraged.

Having practically no money — about $1,000 in cash which they were able to beg and borrow — they knew they could not hope to open their play in a Broadway theatre, so they decided to produce it at the Provincetown Theatre in Greenwich Village. This tiny theatre had the tradition and prestige of having sheltered the

So You Want to Be a Producer? 107

original Provincetown Players, which included Eugene O'Neill, and they would not be faced with union problems and stage-hands.

They built their scenery in a little shop in Brooklyn and had a friend design the scenery for them for a percentage of the profits.

At the time that they produced the show, there were no minimum wage scales for actors set by Actors' Equity. They interviewed hundreds of actors, in the basement of the Union Church, who were willing to gamble on taking tiny salaries at first in the hope of moving uptown with the play and receiving increased salaries. Their cast was composed almost entirely of unknown actors.

They scoured all the second-hand shops in New York for old costumes, properties, furniture, etc.

They each performed a job on the production, without salary. One directed the play. Another handled the publicity, sought theatre parties, and helped with the casting. The other handled all the business details.

They were fortunate enough to open their play at the Provincetown Theatre on an off-night for Broadway. The first-string critics came in curiosity to see what was going on at the little Provincetown, having been bombarded with publicity releases.

Much to everyone's surprise, including the producers, the play came off with stunning force. The production was simple, but ingenious, and the performance extremely sincere.

The next day, the reviews appeared. They were very flattering.

Since it was late in the theatrical season, many Broadway theatres were "dark". As a result, the producers of "Precedent" were immediately deluged with offers to bring the play to Broadway.

The play moved uptown to the Bijou Theatre and ran through the summer. It never did very much business, but it always held its own.

It was all a stroke of luck.

Now for the amusing budget of "Precedent" and explanations of why it can no longer be duplicated:

Building and painting of scenery	$ 300
Costumes	14
Equity Bond	550 (not cash)
Furniture	35
Electrical equipment	50 (Rental)
Salaries to crew	45
Printing of tickets	15
One week's theatre rent in advance	150
Teamster	5
Telephone	14 (deposit)
Petty Cash	32
Typing	16
Mailing	31
Printing programs	35
	$1,292 Total

So You Want to Be a Producer?

The producers were able to persuade a reputable business-man to post a letter-of-guarantee covering the cast salaries, so that none of their precious cash was tied up with Actors' Equity. They were able to engage some actors at salaries as low as $15 a week and the highest salary was $50. (Since that time Equity has established absolute minimums of $25 and $40.)

Being ignorant of union regulations, the producers did not hire a union teamster to haul their furniture. Since they were producing at the Provincetown Theatre, this infringement escaped attention.

They were not required to employ union stagehands at the Provincetown Theatre, but were able to engage friends of theirs who were eager to help in the production and willing to accept a nominal salary of $15 a week shifting scenery in order to get theatrical experience.

Fortunately the play did not require elaborate furniture, so they were able to use "junk".

The cast supplied their own photographs.

No paid advertising was used.

The playwright waived his advance royalties. (Today the Dramatists' Guild expressly forbids this.)

Finally, the entire production was performed in what happened to be the only "little theatre" in New York with any professional standing. Today that famous little playhouse is so down-at-the-heels, as the result of a score of wistful productions that have been presented there since the production of "Precedent", that it is practically impossible to persuade the Broadway critics to attend a performance there.

A "shoe-string" production cannot possibly be produced on Broadway today for anything under $3,000.

"Shoe-string" producing on Broadway requires skilful and experienced management. It usually means that the producer is able to get credit.

Most "shoe-string" productions are outright failures.

WHAT ARE THE ITEMS IN THE OPERATING COST?

Answer: Many of the items in the operating cost are the same as appear on the production cost and have been paid in advance for two weeks by deposits. However, after two weeks, these costs must be paid every week that the play runs and if the play does not take in enough money at the box-office to pay them, then the losses must be met out of the reserve fund, if there is a reserve fund.

Naturally, when the losses continue to accrue, the play must close. Since plays that are badly received the opening night can take in such fantastically low grosses as $300 a week and less than that, producers frequently "fold" a play quickly to salvage at least something out of the wreck.

When a play is politely received and the grosses

So You Want to Be a Producer?

are equally modest, the operating cost must be low for the play to continue.

A typical operating budget for a one-set play is as follows:

Cast Salaries	$1,850	(12 actors)
Advertising	600	(company share of total advertising)
Press Agent	100	
Company Manager	100	
Stage Manager	75	
Asst. Stage Manager	40	
Office Rent, etc.	50	
Secretary	35	
Printing	40	
Electrician	65	
Exploitation	25	(Theatre Party Representative)
Rental electrical equip.	125	
Rental properties	30	
Rental furniture	100	
Insurance	10	
Incidentals	25	
Author's royalties	325	(on $6,000 gross)
	$3,595	Total Operating Cost

You will notice that the author's royalties are calculated on a $6,000 gross. The reason for this is that, on a percentage contract with the theatre owner, the producer usually receives only 60% of the gross receipts. This percentage on a $6,000 gross will give the producer, as his share, a total weekly income at the box-office of $3,600.

In the figures rendered, his costs are $3,595.

As a result, he must do a weekly gross business of $6,000 to break even.

At the time of estimating the production cost, the producer must always calculate his operating cost also and determine at what gross each week he will at least meet his expenses.

The operating budget submitted is a normal one. There are productions which operate for considerably less, but there are many that are much more expensive. The important thing for a producer is to keep his operating costs down, unless he thinks he can bring in an audience by a whirlwind advertising campaign.

It will be noted that in the operating budget quoted, the only stage-hand salary included is for an electrician needed to operate a portable lighting board, since the production required many light changes. The theatre owner always supplies a house crew, consisting of a chief electrician, chief property man, chief carpenter and a curtain man. This crew is held sufficient for a one-set show by the stage-hands' union. But on larger productions, the producer is required to employ many more men.

Salaries in New York range as follows:

Carpenter	$75 a week
Electrician	75 a week
Property man	75 a week
Assistants	65 a week
Boss Flyman	6.75 a performance
Curtain Man	6.75 a performance

Clearers, grips, etc. 8 A. M. to 5 P. M. $1.50 an hour
5 P. M. to 8 A. M. $1.75 " "
Sundays & holidays $2.00 " "

In the case where the producer rents a theatre outright, on a "four wall" basis, he must also include in his operating cost the rental of the theatre and all the expenses and salaries required to operate the theatre, in addition to his company cost. A list of typical theatre expenses has already been given.

WHAT DOES THE PRODUCER DO DURING THE PRODUCTION?

Answer: In the event that he does not direct the play, he concerns himself with booking a theatre, haggling on all costs with scenic builders and painters, costumers, etc. He will argue with the union for a reduced crew. He will be in search of theatre parties and benefits. He will thrash out salaries with actors and their agents. He will be a glorified business manager and publicity man. He will watch rehearsals of the play and make suggestions about the casting and rewriting of the play, if the latter is necessary.

Or he may turn the entire job of producing over to a staff of assistants and simply sign checks. If he likes, he can assign the latter duty to his general manager and not be around at all.

A producer can do as much or as little as he pleases or is able to do.

HOW MUCH DOES A PRODUCER MAKE OUT OF A SUCCESS?

Answer: Before answering that one, let us see how *little* he can make.

In the last few years many pat traditions in the theatre have vanished.

For instance, at one time there was always a steady audience that would patronize any play at the famous Empire Theatre.

Several plays at the Empire Theatre in the last few years have known evenings where the gross receipts were $10 or $15!

There is no in-between any longer in the theatre. Either a play is on top of the heap or on the bottom. Plays that cost $30,000 to produce open to poor reviews and at the end of the first week take in two or three hundred dollars, or *less*. When a play needs approximately $7,000 a week to clear expenses, the losses can be heart-breaking.

Some fool-hardy souls persist in trying to "build up" an attraction after a weak opening. This usually means throwing good money after bad. The public

So You Want to Be a Producer?

will stay away by the thousands from a "flop" and no dint of coaxing will get them in.

You can lose every cent you put into a production and more. Bonds will vanish. Reserve funds will melt away. You will find that you can't even give away the scenery that cost thousands of dollars to build and which may have the paint practically still fresh! In fact, you will find that it will cost you money to get the crew to take the scenery out of the theatre. And it will cost you still more money to have it hauled away to a dumping ground to be burned! Or, if you want to hang on to the stuff, you can put it in a warehouse and pay monthly storage charges.

But you want to know what a producer can make out of a success. Well, he can make an amazing lot of money.

In fact, there is no other speculation in the world that can bring you so big a return on your initial investment as producing a successful play, not even Wall Street.

Huge theatrical profits, however, are only obtained when the producer is shrewd and hard-hitting in his deals. He must keep down his operating costs at all hazards, as low as possible. The production cost does not matter so much, although the less expensive the better, if the production does not suffer. However, it is on low operating costs that weekly profits come. The production cost is written off by these weekly profits until the show is "out of the red". Some plays can be "off the nut" in two or three weeks. Most successful plays show a clear profit at the end of ten or twelve weeks.

With the Broadway run, road companies, foreign companies, stock rights, picture rights, etc., a smash-hit play can net a profit of anywhere from $250,000 to $5,000,000! When the producer has outside backing his profits are usually split 50–50 with the "angel". Sometimes he has to give away more, sometimes less. The producer will frequently write himself in for a weekly salary while the play is running, adding to his personal receipts.

Of all the plays produced each season along Broadway, about ten per cent. make money and about ten per cent. break even. When you gamble in the theatre, it's five to one against you. However, you can produce five successive plays and they may all be failures!

But when you do "hit it on the nose", you can make enough money out of one success to last you for the rest of your life.

You can break your heart trying to hit it.

WHAT IS THE BIGGEST HURDLE IN PRODUCING?

Answer: There are no two ways about this one. It's the opening night. That first performance is make or break for the show.

There was a time in the theatre when a producer

could have his show received coolly at the première, or even hooted out of court, and proceed, notwithstanding, to a long engagement and rich profits through sensational publicity and promotion methods. "East Is West" and "Abie's Irish Rose" are two classics in this tradition.

That day in the theatre is gone. Only occasionally now does a freak success such as "Tobacco Road" develop after an indifferent première.

The highly developed talking-picture has had a great deal to do with heightening the demands of an audience upon the theatre. As a result, the customer who pays six dollars or more for a pair of theatre seats wants something extremely good for his money.

Consequently, the producer puts all his chips on the opening night. And that Broadway audience of professional first-nighters is a tough and cruel body to get past. They love their favorites, yes, but they are cold, jaded, and difficult to suit. When they do like a show, though, they go the whole hog and the word spreads like wildfire around town that you have a hit.

Most important are the reviews. While flattering or kind reviews won't help a weak play, adverse notices will ruin practically any show. And unqualified "rave" notices spell fame and fortune.

HOW EXPRESSLY DO "RAVE" NOTICES HELP A SHOW?

Answer: In the first place, items of praise from the reviews are always quoted by the producer in his advertisements. High praise from the critics is the major authoritative endorsement for a play.

More directly, the theatre is supported largely by what is called the "carriage trade" and visitors to New York. These two classes of theatre patrons usually purchase their tickets through the Broadway ticket agencies.

The men who own the agencies rely on the critics to inform them if a play is good. Thus, when they receive a call for tickets to a "good" new show, they recommend the plays that have won the approval of the critics. The first few weeks in the life of a play are highly important. Through those early audiences the word of mouth begins to spread. The ticket-brokers are extremely important in bringing in those early audiences.

Frequently, when the brokers read in the papers that a show is a "smash", they approach the producer and negotiate a "buy", whereby they guarantee the producer to sell all or a certain portion of his tickets over a contracted period of weeks. Naturally, they sell these blocks of tickets at a premium, though they buy them from the producer at the box-office price. Sometimes the producer, if he is a tough business-man, will get a cut of the profit they make on the sale of each ticket, perhaps 25¢ or 50¢ on each ticket. This extra profit is called the "ice".

In many cases of solid successes, however, the box-office treasurers, old and seasoned hands at the game and thoroughly acquainted with the "boys" who act as ticket-brokers, cut in on this "ice". Many $60-a-week box-office treasurers have become comparatively rich in this fashion.

There is also the Public Ticket Service, founded by Joe Leblang, and located in the basement of Grey's Drug Store on 7th Avenue and 43rd Street. The Leblang trade is largely a cut-rate business, designed to help those productions which have enjoyed only a luke warm reception. Leblang's sells tickets at half price and frequently can sell enough tickets for a producer to keep a show going when the operating costs are low. The Leblang trade has diminished sadly in recent years.

Getting past that opening night is the real goal for any production. Even the Theatre Guild, which has a guaranteed subscription audience, counts on the critics and good reviews to help a show after the subscription period is ended.

DO PRODUCERS USE THEIR OWN MONEY?
Answer: Only occasionally.

The seasoned producer is always aware of how hazardous a gamble the business of producing a play can be. As a result, he usually seeks at least partial outside financing for a production.

There are times when a producer is thoroughly sold

on a play, but can't get anyone to share his conviction and will finance it entirely himself. Only a few producers are willing to gamble all or nothing on a play, that is, take all the profits or all the losses. This occurs usually when the producer is independently rich or has just enjoyed the returns from an enormous hit and wants to pyramid his profits on another production.

Your prudent producer, however, is prone to let someone else put up the money and receive fifty per cent. of the potential net profits for his services.

The majority of producers are so fixed that they need outside money to do a show. Only a handful of producers are independently rich.

WHERE DO YOU GET BACKING?

Answer: Outside of having a rich uncle, there are three methods:

1. "Promoting" some business-man or any independent person with money and a mind to gamble on a play. This is the subject for a three-act farce-comedy and requires no further comment here.

2. Through a motion picture company. Most of the major motion picture companies depend on the theatre for material and will back a play if they think it is potentially a successful motion picture. All of the major companies have New York offices and story editors who consider manuscripts submitted by producers looking for financing.

So You Want to Be a Producer?

Motion Picture Company Eastern Story Editors

Paramount, Russell Holman, 1501 Broadway
Metro-Goldwyn-Mayer, Bertram Bloch, 1540 Broadway
Fox-20th Century, Robert Bassler, 30 Rockefeller Plaza
RKO, Lillian Messinger, 1270 6th Avenue
Warner Brothers, Jacob Wilk, 321 West 44th Street
Columbia, Richard Aldrich, 729 7th Avenue
Universal, Charles Beahan, 30 Rockefeller Plaza

Picture companies will usually finance only well established managers with successful records. Arthur Hopkins, Sam H. Harris, George Abbott, and Max Gordon are among those producers who have been financed by picture companies. Occasionally, a tyro can win motion picture money for his production by dint of having a promising manuscript and a good sales approach. Although, even in this latter case, the producer usually needs at least some Broadway experience. Alex Yokel and Theron Bamberger, two former press agents, were able to obtain picture money for the productions of "Three Men on a Horse" and "Fly Away Home", even though they had practically no previous experience as producers.

3. There are two firms in the theatre that act as bankers for producers, Lee Shubert and the Leblang Cut Rate Ticket organization. Mr. Shubert happens to own a great many theatres. As a result, he frequently invests money in other producers' productions in or-

der to book an attraction. The Leblang office, founded by the late Joe Leblang, is run by Matty Zimmerman. This latter organization also owns several theatres which need attractions occasionally and in addition there is always the consideration of the cut-rate business. If a manager has his show geared low on the operating cost, Zimmerman will sometimes invest money in the production either for tickets, a share of the profits, or for both.

If you have never produced a show before and are not known along Broadway, you will have to dig up your backing independently. That puts you in class one and the previous reference to farce-comedy still holds.

WHAT DOES IT COST TO BOOK A THEATRE?
Answer: The subject of a theatre contract is one of the trickiest problems that confronts a producer.

There are two ways of booking a theatre:

1. On a percentage basis.
2. On a "four wall" basis.

The percentage basis is one by which a producer brings his play into a theatre on a contract whereby he shares the weekly gross receipts with the theatre owner. The usual terms are 60–40 on the first $7,000, which means the producer receives $4,200 on that sum. When the gross is above this figure, the percentage may vary every additional two or three thou-

So You Want to Be a Producer?

sand dollars at 65–35, 70–30, etc. In consideration of this percentage arrangement, the theatre owner supplies the producer with a certain number of the stagehands required for the play, depending on how many sets the production has, a share of the advertising costs, box-office help, ushers, cleaners, door-men, etc.

The theatre owner always places what is called a "stop-clause" in the contract. That is, if the gross receipts fall below a stated figure, at which the attraction is no longer profitable to the house, the theatre owner has the right to give the producer notice to vacate. This is intended for the protection of the theatre owner who may be housing an attraction which has such low operating costs that it can afford to stay open at a low gross which gives the theatre owner no profit. Since another attraction may come knocking at the theatre door, the owner wants to be in a position where he can book the other attraction. Four thousand dollars is about the lowest "stop" figure a theatre owner will grant a producer and $7,000 is the average figure.

In these days of ludicrously low gross receipts for failures, the theatre owner frequently demands from a producer a cash guarantee of the house expenses, viz.: salaries for crew, box-office help, ushers, advertising, etc. These costs run between $1,200 and $2,500 a week, exclusive of rent, depending on the size of the producer's production.

The drawing up of a percentage contract is always an involved business, even though the form of the contract itself is usually brief and seemingly simple. It is always advisable to engage a business-manager expert in the ins and outs of a theatre contract, or an experienced theatrical attorney.

If a play only grosses a few hundred dollars the first week after it opens, it is apparent that the theatre owner will not even cover his expenses unless they are guaranteed in cash by the producer. Occasionally the producer is able to convince the theatre owner that he has a good show, or he may have a notable cast or star commanding a certain box-office drawing power. In such a case, the theatre owner is sometimes satisfied with a "first money" guarantee. That is, the producer guarantees to the theatre owner the first receipts until the theatre owner's expenses are covered.

When a manager leases a theatre on a "four-wall" basis, he rents the theatre and pays all the expenses necessary to operate the house out of his own pocket. Theatre rentals run from as low as $400 a week up to $2,500 a week. Under such an arrangement, the producer pays a flat sum to the theatre owner and pays all the help himself. Thus, if the house expenses are $1,200 a week, rent $500 a week, and the cost of operating the show $4,500, the producer must take in a gross of $6,200 to break even, to quote some arbitrary,

So You Want to Be a Producer? 125

but average, figures. Anything over this gross is clear profit to the producer, if he has rented the house on a "four wall" basis. On a percentage contract, the producer does not enjoy this advantage, nor does he take the risk.

Theatre terms vary with the time of the year. If there are a great many plays in rehearsals, terms are naturally stiff. In the spring, theatre terms are usually inviting because production is slack. A good season is one when things are booming, plenty of hits, big grosses, lots of productions. In a good season theatre terms become difficult for the manager and fine for the theatre owner. But nobody cares very much then, for producers and theatre owners are making money.

HOW MUCH MONEY CAN A PRODUCER MAKE ON TOUR?

Answer: Rumor would have it that the road is dead. It's indubitably true that the mellow days when a producer could send out half a dozen carbon copies of his New York success and reap tremendous profits on the road are gone. But there is still some gold left in the provinces.

The trouble with sending a play out on tour is the railroading. Many of the old legitimate theatres have gone permanently "dark" or have become motion picture houses. As a result, a manager finds it difficult to plot an itinerary for his touring production without making long jumps from one stand to the next.

In the last few years the road seems to have been revived considerably. Katharine Cornell's recent famous tour across the continent and back brought out huge and profitable audiences. Billy Rose, of "Jumbo" fame, sent out a touring revue and played the most isolated towns to large profits. New York successes with their original casts have gone on the road and been received favorably in the key cities such as Boston, Philadelphia, Chicago, Washington, etc. Several companies of both "Tobacco Road" and "Three Men on a Horse" have enjoyed amazing success on tour.

But when it is all added up, the expenses involved and the natural hazards of touring a play are still somewhat discouraging. The big money is in New York. A touring production that nets a profit of $75,000 for a producer after a season of trouping is just about tops for the field. This is not a profit to be sneezed at, but it does not compare to the profit the same production can show on the producer's books after a successful season in New York.

HOW DOES A PRODUCER SHARE IN PICTURE RIGHTS?

Answer: This is a question that has assumed major proportions in recent years since the advent of the talking picture. It was the subject for a recent storm of controversy between the producers and the playwrights.

Until recently, a producer was entitled to 50% of the motion picture sale if he kept the play running for three weeks in New York or for 75 consecutive performances on the road. The producer and the author shared jointly in paying the commissions of the playbroker and the Arbiter, the latter being empowered by the Dramatists' Guild to consummate all picture sales for the author and producer.

But a growing disposition on the part of motion picture companies to finance Broadway producers finally led to revolt on the part of the members of the Dramatists' Guild on the grounds that a picture company financing a production could dictate the amount of the picture sale and that the producer was a partner with the picture company and consequently could not possibly represent the author fairly in transacting a picture sale.

Leading playwrights, organized firmly and powerfully in the Dramatists' Guild, met in closed conference and formulated a new Minimum Basic Agreement for the sale of a play to a producer, with an express clause covering the disposition of picture rights.

The new dictum on the sale of picture rights allows the producer only 40% of the picture sale. Thus, on a sale of $50,000, whereas the producer formerly received $25,000, he now receives only $20,000.

The producer still must keep his play running for three weeks in New York or 75 consecutive performances on the road in order to share in picture rights at all.

IS THERE ANY PRODUCERS' ASSOCIATION?
Answer: The answer to this question is discovered in the material immediately foregoing, where it is explained how the Dramatists' Guild forced a new Minimum Basic Agreement down the managerial throats. Whether right or wrong is beside the point. The fact remains that the producers were in no position to fight back against the organized authors.

The producers are pitifully unorganized. Pitiful, that is, for the theatre as a whole. There are two managerial organizations, one the New York League of Theatres and the other an offshoot of that body, the National Association of the Legitimate Theatre. The former was formed principally to combat ticket-scalping and has just about as much power and influence as the latter body — none.

Producers have always been selfish creatures in the history of the Broadway theatre and they have never been able to band together effectively for a common good. They were licked hands down when the actors went on strike and formed Actors' Equity and they have always been more or less powerless to fight back against the powerfully organized stage-hands. Their only weapon is the right to abandon producing, a sorry weapon indeed.

There are individual producers who have the inter-

So You Want to Be a Producer?

est of the theatre at heart and would like to see an effective producers' association formed, but, by and large, the successful producer runs alone, not with the pack.

The actors are organized, the playwrights are organized, the stage-hands are organized, the scene designers are organized, the musicians are organized, the teamsters are organized, even the bill-posters, ushers and valets are organized, but not the producers.

When you become a producer, you are in a class by yourself.

WHO HAVE BECOME PRODUCERS?

Answer: The answer harks back to the fact that anyone can become a producer. But among the more established producers, there are some interesting backgrounds that can be noted briefly.

Men like William A. Brady, Lee Shubert, Sam Harris, and Al Woods grew up in the theatre. They began way back in the 10-20-30 days as prize-fight managers, box-office treasurers, coat-room boys, and what not. They are viewed with affection as the "old-line managers".

Several playwrights have become producers, including Elmer Rice, George Abbott, Albert Bein, Lawrence Langner, etc.

Press agents have often turned producer; witness Jed Harris, Herman Shumlin, Alex Yokel, Theron Bamberger, Arthur Hopkins, Brock Pemberton, etc.

Stage managers have become directors and subsequently producers, as for example, Murray Queen, Worthington Minor, Guthrie McClintic, Alfred de Liagre, Jr., Forrest Haring, etc.

Many independently rich business men, sometimes hailing from Wall Street, have become producers, viz.: Dwight Deere Wiman, Rowland Stebbins, Richard Aldrich, Harry Moses, James Ullman, Crosby Gaige, etc.

You never know in the theatre when you may be talking to a potential producer. They come from the most unexpected places.

HOW MANY PRODUCERS ARE THERE IN NEW YORK?

Answer: Approximately 100 people can be listed as active managers, meaning they have produced more than one play and give evidence of intending to stay in the business of producing.

IS THERE ROOM FOR MORE PRODUCERS?

Answer: One of the more pleasant aspects of the Broadway theatre is the fact that there is always room for another success. The more hits on Broadway, the better for the theatre as a whole. The theatre seems extremely attractive to audiences when they can go to see plays several times a week and consistently be entertained.

The theatre can always use a competent and sincere producer.

WHAT DOES IT COST TO MAINTAIN AN OFFICE?

Answer: This is a not unimportant point, since a producer can go for a long time without doing a show. When a producer is inactive, he is faced with overhead and no income.

The major items to be considered in running a theatrical producing office are rent, telephone and telegraph, postage, replenishing of stationery, salary for a secretary, and salary for a play-reader. The last is optional with a producer, but the others are "musts." In addition, a producer may carry other people on his staff, from an office-boy to a general manager.

A conservative weekly budget for an office is as follows:

Rent	$15	
Telephone	10	(a producer's 'phone bill can be staggering)
Secretary	25	
Playreader	25	(or by the manuscript)
Postage	5	
Incidentals	5	(towel service, stationery, spring water, etc.)
	$85 Total	

Many producers find it costs them several times that amount to maintain an office. But even $85 is a tidy little sum to be paying out every week in the hope of finding a play to produce.

WHAT DOES A PRODUCER DO WHEN HE IS NOT PRODUCING?

Answer: If he is really interested in the theatre or in making a living out of it, he will find plenty to do.

His major task, as already noted in detail, will be to find good manuscripts. This may mean frequent consultations with playwrights, advising them, encouraging them, even giving them financial aid. He will always be searching for something that will make a good play, whether it be a book, a story, an idea, or perhaps something in the news headlines.

He will see other plays regularly so that he can become acquainted with new actors and have a line on their ability. In this connection, he will keep careful casting files and interview actors regularly even though he may have no immediate production plans.

He will interview new designers, technicians, directors, stage managers. He will always be searching for people of talent who can bring something to his next production.

Under these conditions, being a producer is a full-time job.

SECTION IV

SO YOU WANT TO BE A DIRECTOR?

"The worst element to contribute to a conversation is agreement. Obviously, believing all you say does not even swing in the direction of an interesting contradiction. Of course you are right, and you know it and I know it, and if there is anything to be gained I gladly acknowledge it."

— PHILIP MOELLER, *Theatre Guild director, to the author, after a general discussion of the points of this section*

SO YOU WANT TO BE A DIRECTOR?

Answer: Directing a play is easily the most fascinating job in the theatre. Directing is creative work and encompasses the whole joy of "putting on a show".

It is also a talent that defies discussion.

A director approaching a producer who has never seen him direct is at a total loss to define his ability.

You can say, "I'm a swell director." Or, if you think exaggeration will help, you can add, "In fact, I am a genius."

Unfortunately, that won't prove it, any more than being modest by saying, "I think I can direct a play", is likely to help you.

The only way a director can prove anything about himself is by directing a play.

The talent of a director is best measured by watching him at work, or by seeing a play that he has directed. You can't *talk* a good game of directing, you have to *do* it.

Try it on yourself, if you think you're a director. Can you explain *why* you think you're good, other than by using generalizations? Can you describe specifically *how* you directed a play successfully, if you are making your explanations to someone who did not see the play you staged?

HOW DO YOU GET STARTED?

Answer: A famous producer was once approached in his office by a young man who asked him for a chance to direct a play. The young man admitted he had never before directed a play on Broadway, but pointed out he had staged several ambitious productions at college. He believed he was a pretty good director and said so. The producer listened to him for a while, unimpressed, and finally remarked that he wouldn't think of entrusting a production of his to an unknown director.

"Well, how can I get started?" the young man asked earnestly.

"I don't know," replied the producer coldly. "Why don't you produce a play and direct it yourself?"

That's the easiest way of getting started on Broadway as a director. If you're a producer, you can be your own boss and hire yourself to direct.

If you can find a good manuscript and bring it to a producer, he may let you direct it in return for the favor.

Another way to start as a director is to form a summer theatre company of your own, or else get a job directing in a summer theatre. It may lead to a Broadway directing job, if some producer should happen to see and like your work.

The more practical method, however, is to get a job as a stage manager and attach yourself to a pro-

So You Want to Be a Director?

ducing firm. After you have served your apprenticeship as a stage manager for a year or two, you may be able to persuade the producer you work for to take a chance on allowing you to direct a play for him, particularly if he happens to like your way of thinking and working around a theatre and the office.

Another method of getting a directing job in New York is to acquire a reputation in some leading little theatre group. But your chances for getting a job on Broadway this way are slim. The Broadway producers have very little regard for amateurs.

HOW DOES A DIRECTOR WIN A REPUTATION?

Answer: By directing successful plays.

Direct a *money-maker* and your name will be surrounded with magic.

Direct a bad play and your reputation suffers. It won't matter how valiantly you have labored with your cast, or how adroit you have been in handling the technical production, if the play is a "turkey". Either your efforts as a director will be ignored, or, worse yet, you may be accused of having done a bad job. Broadway has a neat knack of lauding a director for a success and damning him for a failure. Bad plays offer small opportunity for good directing.

The distinction between good directing and bad playwriting is not always made in the Broadway scheme of things.

If you are asked to direct a play and you think the manuscript is hopeless, you will be wise not to direct that play. The fee you may receive will not be worth the damage done to your reputation as a director through the failure of the play.

No director can do a really good job on a bad manuscript.

Item, reputations are made by doing a *good* directing job on a *good* play.

WHO ARE THE PEOPLE WHO DIRECT PLAYS?
Answer: There are some people in the Broadway theatre who think anybody can direct a play. Occasionally people of this opinion have attempted to direct plays, only to discover that it is far from simple. Unfortunately there is no one to stop them from trying.

The fact of the matter is that directing a play requires a very special talent. Either you are a director, or you are not.

The Broadway theatre does not attach the kind of importance to the province of directing that is to be found in the Continental theatre where the director is often referred to as the *régisseur,* a title that has genuine significance. In Europe, no one dares to become a director before having had years of general theatre training. But along Broadway, people completely unequipped to direct a play try their hand at it, invariably with dismal results.

Generally speaking, the ranks of the Broadway di-

So You Want to Be a Director?

rectors are composed of three broad groups, free-lance directors, producers, and authors and actors.

HOW MANY PRODUCERS DIRECT THEIR OWN PRODUCTIONS?

Answer: Answering this question in reverse, the fact is that there are comparatively few free-lance directors on Broadway; that is, directors who make their living in the theatre entirely out of staging plays for those producers who engage outside directors.

Many directors who win a reputation become producers.

Among the established producers who direct their own productions are Arthur Hopkins, Jed Harris, Brock Pemberton, Herman Shumlin, Robert Milton, Chester Erskin, Theodore Hammerstein, George Abbott, Richard Herndon, William Harris, Jr., Walter Hart, Leo Bulgakov, Guthrie McClintic, Gilbert Miller, John Golden, Frank Merlin, H. C. Potter, Alfred de Liagre, Jr., Walter Hartwig, Gustav Blum, William Friedlander and Bela Blau.

Philip Moeller of the Theatre Guild board is a director and stages many of the Guild's productions.

All three members of the board of the Group Theatre — Harold Clurman, Lee Strasberg, and Cheryl Crawford — are directors and take turns at directing the Group productions.

In fact, scratch a Broadway producer and you are likely to find a director.

So You Want to Go Into the Theatre?

WHAT PRODUCERS DO NOT DIRECT THEIR OWN PRODUCTIONS?

Answer: Fortunately for the free-lance directors, there are a goodly number of producers who do not direct.

Among the established producers who engage directors for their productions are Sam H. Harris, Lee Shubert, William Brady, Sr., Phillip Dunning, Dwight Deere Wiman, Rowland Stebbins, Al Woods, Courtney Burr, Crosby Gaige, Sam Grisman, Harry Moses, Morris Gest, Max Gordon, Frederick Ayer, Thomas Kilpatrick, Sidney Harmon, Tom Weatherly, Henry Forbes, James Ullman, Bushar and Tuerk, Alex Yokel, Elizabeth Miehle, Eddie Dowling, Raymond Moore, Lawrence Weber, and Laurence Schwab.

But many of these producers have associations and affiliations with certain directors that tend to limit the chances for an outsider.

For instance, George Kaufman is a silent partner with Sam Harris and directs many of the firm's productions; Miriam Doyle is a member of Rowland Stebbins' staff and directs many of his plays; Robert Sinclair is general stage director for Max Gordon; Melvyn Douglas directs frequently for Bushar and Tuerk; Guthrie McClintic directs all of Katharine Cornell's productions, being her husband and partner; A. H. Van Beuren has been directing plays for Al Woods for many years; Dwight Deere Wiman has an association

So You Want to Be a Director?

with Auriol Lee, the British director; Sam Woods directs for George M. Cohan, etc.

Directors who establish themselves by directing a successful production for a producer usually continue to direct plays for that producer. There are many such friendships and affiliations between producers and directors which make it bewilderingly difficult for a newcomer to get a chance.

WHAT SALARY DOES A DIRECTOR EARN?

Answer: Relatively speaking, the director is the most poorly paid of all the workers in the professional theatre, despite the fact that the work he does is of extreme importance.

The standard fee, if there is any at all, for directing a play is $500 a week for the duration of the rehearsal and "try-out" period, which may last four or five weeks.

Occasionally a director will do a show for a flat fee of $2,000. Some very prominent directors can command higher fees, but $3,000 is about the top figure a director gets for directing a play.

On the other hand, directing fees can be as low as $1,000 or $500. Some directors will work for nothing, because they think directing the play will bring them a reputation.

Frequently, directors receive a small percentage of the gross receipts for the run of the play, in addition to their fee. This percentage is seldom more than ½% or 1% of the gross receipts, so that on a successful play a director may receive between $50 and $100 a week in additional revenue as long as the play is running. The director will usually receive an additional small percentage on each road company the producer sends out.

On certain very rare occasions, a director will perform his services for a "piece of the show", whereby he shares in the producer's profits.

The simple fact of the matter is that there is precious little money to be made out of directing plays, certainly not in proportion to the salaries paid to leading actors, or the royalties and profits realized by successful authors and producers.

Even if you direct four plays a season, a high average, you are not likely to earn much more than $10,000 a year, despite the fact that you may work for weeks in advance of rehearsing each production and despite the fact that you are entrusted with the fate of each production.

That's why most successful directors on Broadway become producers.

WHEN IS A DIRECTOR PAID?

Answer: The usual procedure is for a producer to give a director a check at the end of each week of rehearsal.

Some directors insist on receiving their first week's salary in advance of signing a contract to direct a play.

So You Want to Be a Director?

This is done because sometimes directors devote weeks of effort to casting a play for a producer and consulting with the author on the manuscript, only to have the producer abandon production for any number of reasons!

Directors who obtain a percentage of the gross receive their checks within seven days after the end of each week, or else they see a lawyer.

WHAT KIND OF A CONTRACT DOES A DIRECTOR SIGN?

Answer: There is no standard contract for a director, although Actors' Equity provides a contract form on request.

On some occasions, the contract between producer and director is merely verbal, depending on how well they know each other. A director who forms this kind of an agreement is a trusting soul.

One simple form of contract for a director is a letter from the producer addressed to him wherein all the terms of the agreement are stated. By signing his acceptance on the bottom of this letter, it becomes a binding contract.

The most advisable contract for a director is one which any good theatrical lawyer will draw up for him.

IS THERE A DIRECTORS' UNION?

Answer: Like the producers, with whom the directors, as a class, are allied, the Broadway directors have no organization of their own.

To begin with, there are not very many free-lance directors along Broadway, certainly not more than 50 all told and, of this number, perhaps only a dozen have any reputation and work frequently.

Quaintly enough, the director's best protective weapon is his talent. He performs a highly specialized kind of work in the theatre and can always walk out on a play should the producer fail to pay him. As a result, a director who has both ability and a reputation is not likely to suffer much abuse.

In any event, the free-lance directors have never bothered to band together as an organized group. If you come into the theatre as a director, you will be on your own, for better or worse.

WHAT IS A DIRECTOR'S RELATIONSHIP TO A PRODUCER?

Answer: This is another question that requires two general answers.

1. No trouble.

2. Trouble, trouble, trouble.

It all depends upon how active the producer wants to be in the production and upon his temperament.

There are some producers who give the director *carte blanche* on a production, satisfied that the man they have engaged to direct the production is fully competent to do the job his own way. In such cases, the director does all the casting and merely refers the actors to the producer to settle their salaries and sign

So You Want to Be a Director?

their contracts, after consulting with the author on all final selections. Likewise, he stages the entire production and supervises all selections of costumes, furniture, properties, etc. In these happy circumstances, about all the producer does for the director is to pay the bills.

But there are other cases when the director must consult with the producer on every item of the production. If they see eye to eye on things and can come to agreements after reasonable discussion, everything is pleasant.

On the other hand, it may be touch and go between producer and director on each little detail, until both are utterly worn out and exhausted from arguing. The producer may insist on casting the play his own way. He may attend all rehearsals and insist on an active voice in the staging of the production and the revising of the manuscript. In short, he may make a hell of a lot of trouble for the director.

The point is that the director, in the final analysis, is an employee of the producer. If he doesn't like the circumstances that surround his job, he can either lump it or quit. Which is another reason why many successful directors become producers.

DOES A DIRECTOR SUPERVISE THE LIGHTING OF A SHOW?

Answer: Lighting a show is one of the most important tasks in the final stages of rehearsal of a production.

It isn't necessary for the director to light the show himself, but he should know something about it.

If the director is a specialist on the subject, he may do the job himself, working with the chief electrician.

However, usually the scene designer takes over this assignment, after consulting with the director. On some productions, a special lighting expert is called in by the producer.

ARE THERE ANY AGENTS FOR DIRECTORS?

Answer: Some of the casting agents represent directors, since it is often quite logical for a casting agent who is recommending actors to a producer to suggest a director, as well.

A good director usually doesn't need an agent, since the field is limited and a man with a reputation will be sent for by a producer seeking a director.

There is a typical Broadway procedure, whereby, when a director hears that a producer intends doing a certain play, he will dash around to that producer's office and volunteer his services ecstatically, even though he has never even read the play!

DOES A DIRECTOR NEED EXPERIENCE AS AN ACTOR?

Answer: That depends largely on your method of directing.

If your style is to teach an actor his performance by rote, you should be able to act the part out for him.

If, however, you direct a performance through ex-

So You Want to Be a Director?

plaining the play to your cast and are content to let them create their own performances, you need not be an experienced actor yourself. Many excellent directors have never done any acting and would probably be bad actors if they tried!

But, in the final analysis, the fully-rounded director should know something about every department in the production of a play, and it is to his advantage if he happens to be an actor himself.

SHOULD A DIRECTOR BE ABLE TO REWRITE A PLAY?

Answer: He certainly should be able to suggest changes in a play to the author, when they are necessary.

Since it is the express task of a director to translate an author's play into terms of an acting performance for an audience, he ought to know more than a little about the business of constructing a play.

There's an old adage around the theatre that plays are not written, but rewritten. A good director is a fine director if he can sit down to a manuscript and help with the revisions. Even extremely successful and important playwrights can be helped by a director in the rewriting of manuscripts.

DOES YOUR AGE MATTER?

Answer: No.

In the Broadway theatre a young director can be just as successful as one who is hoary-headed, although a youngster fresh out of college is not likely to be taken as seriously at first as a director who has had years of experience and an impressive record of achievement.

If you have talent as a director and can get started in the theatre, your youth will not be a handicap.

Robert Sinclair, Worthington Minor, Michael Blankfort, Joe Losey, Robert Rossum, Sidney Salkow, Robert Ross, Anthony Brown, Sidney Kingsley, H. C. Potter, Chester Erskin, Arthur Sircom, Lester Fuller, Bretaigne Windust, Joshua Logan, and Walter Hart are all young men who have directed Broadway productions in recent years. Most of this group are men still in their twenties.

It should be of interest to examine how these directors started in the theatre.

Robert Sinclair, Anthony Brown, Bretaigne Windust, Worthington Minor, Sidney Salkow and Joshua Logan began as stage managers.

Michael Blankfort, Lester Fuller, Walter Hart, Robert Rossum and H. C. Potter began by producing.

Chester Erskin, Arthur Sircom, Robert Ross and Sidney Kingsley began as actors.

WHAT IS A "DIRECTOR'S HOLIDAY"?

Answer: This term is commonly applied to a manuscript that affords the director a virtuoso opportunity. It usually means a play that requires an elaborate and flashy production, intricate timing and pacing, brilliant effects, and a general chance for imaginative staging.

So You Want to Be a Director?

This kind of a production is sharply contrasted with a play that requires only a quiet and simple production, perhaps limited to a single setting and a small cast, relying on mood and subtlety for effectiveness.

Often a director is mistakenly praised in the Broadway theatre for the work of a scene designer or a brilliant lighting expert. Don't be deceived by such a production when you see one. The director may have had very little to do with the elaborate effects. A play that has many swift-moving sets of scenery is not always a well-directed production. The real job of the director is to get a performance out of his cast. The technical production should concern him, certainly, but not to the exclusion of everything else.

But, on the practical side, if you can get a job directing a play that demands a spectacular production, you're "one up" on Broadway, especially if your technical staff is expert.

WHAT DOES DIRECTING LEAD TO?

Answer: A good free-lance director can earn at least a comfortable living and enjoy both the prestige and satisfaction of staging memorable productions. It's an honorable and highly respected craft in the theatre.

Furthermore, as noted frequently in the foregoing, a successful director can become a producer.

Finally, some successful directors are called to Hollywood and earn fabulous salaries for directing talking pictures. However, it is of note that only a handful of Broadway stage directors have "made good" in Hollywood. Directing pictures is not the same as directing a play and requires a different approach and temperament. Only a few stage directors have been able to bridge the gap between the two mediums.

The hysterical boom days of talking pictures are over and Hollywood is no longer searching frantically for directors who can teach actors how to talk.

SECTION V

SO YOU WANT TO BE A SCENE DESIGNER?

"I have always felt that a designer gets what he deserves. If he charges what he thinks he is worth, he should be satisfied, although naturally it is hard for him to get along on the fees of only two productions a season. As for little theatre experience being of no value to a designer on Broadway, you are all wrong. That is the way I started."

— DONALD OENSLAGER, *successful Broadway designer, in a reply to a letter from the author*

SO YOU WANT TO BE A SCENE DESIGNER?
Answer: Being a scene designer connotes that you are something of an artist and are possessed of a fairly sensitive temperament.

Well, Broadway is far from a haven for poets. To be part and parcel of Broadway, one should have a good healthy ego and be perfectly willing to expose himself to the screaming clamor that goes hand in hand with "show business".

Yet, curiously enough, Broadway has been receptive to fine delicate things. Robert Edmond Jones, unquestionably a poet, was able to succeed as a Broadway stage designer and remain untouched by the hue and cry of the commercial theatre.

The modern theatre offers a medium of creative expression to the stage designer. Its dècor grows more imaginative and more beautiful each season. Perhaps the finest elements the theatre has ever known have been contributed to it in recent years by scene designers working for Broadway producers.

One does not have to know anything about the composition, depth, and tectonic brilliance of painting to recognize when a picture is beautiful. Similarly, in the Broadway theatre, scene designers have been able to command broad popular attention with lovely creative stage pictures. Anyone can appreciate an exquisite set of scenery.

At least that's one side of scene designing — for the rest, the facts speak for themselves.

HOW DO YOU BEGIN AS A SCENE DESIGNER?

Answer: You must be admitted to the United Scenic Artists union before you can begin to work as a scene designer in the professional theatre.

The United Scenic Artists became a member of the American Federation of Labor in 1918. Local 829, with offices and clubrooms at 251 West 42nd Street, represents the district of New York and the eastern states.

The union is composed of some 350-odd members, of whom about 60 are designers. The balance are scene painters and studio workers. No scene painter or studio worker may execute his services for a designer who is not a member of the union.

The union was formed to protect its members by creating a standard minimum contract for scenic work in the theatre and to provide for a closed shop.

HOW DO YOU JOIN THE UNION?

Answer: Unlike the actor who, upon being engaged by a producer for a part in a play, automatically becomes a member of Actors' Equity, you cannot work for a producer as a scene designer until the United

So You Want to Be a Scene Designer? 155

Scenic Artists has passed judgment on you and admitted you to membership in its ranks.

Getting into the union is a difficult business.

The bulk of the membership in the United Scenic Artists local 829 consists of men who are merely artisans and laborers. Only a minority of the membership is composed of actual scene designers. As a result, the member scene designers find it very difficult to effect liberal new union legislation in common meeting.

The general feeling in the union is that the ranks of the Broadway theatre are already too crowded with scenic artists.

Consequently, the method of new membership in the union is designed largely to keep people out.

If, however, you are determined to become a scenic designer, you must first visit the union office and express your intention to one of the officers. You will probably be given a long and discouraging tale on how difficult it is to become a member and how slim your chances are on Broadway at best.

Finally, if you persist, you will be told that you are required to pass an examination, given by the union's board of examiners, calling for a knowledge not only of stage drawing and design, but also carpentry, lighting, the history of art and the theatre, etc.

This examination is given once or twice a year and you will be told that you will be informed of the date of the examination. It's advisable to make frequent inquiries, after your initial interview, concerning the exact day on which the examination is scheduled, if you are studying for it and have a great deal of ground to cover. You can take the examination as often as you wish.

In the event that you pass the examination, you must pay an initiation fee of $500 before you can be admitted to the union as a scene designer. Dues are $4 a month and you can be suspended if you are in arrears.

WHAT IF A PRODUCER BECOMES INTERESTED IN YOUR WORK?

Answer: If you are not a member of the union, it won't do you much good. You must be admitted before you can design plays on Broadway.

However, even after you are admitted to the union, you will have to persuade a producer that you have talent. Difficult as it is to be admitted to the union, membership does not guarantee you work. Union membership merely gives you the right to work!

WHAT KIND OF A CONTRACT DO YOU SIGN WITH A PRODUCER?

Answer: The standard contract form provided by the United Scenic Artists. No other form of agreement may be used. A copy of each contract must be filed with the union.

The contract provides a minimum scale of $250 per

So You Want to Be a Scene Designer? 157

design for each setting on a play and no less than $100 for each design on a musical production.

The producer must guarantee the designer program credit under the names of the author and director of the play.

He also guarantees that no alterations will be made in the scenery without the designer's express consent.

In addition, he guarantees to the designer the services of a master carpenter, master property man and master electrician for a period of one week prior to the opening performance.

The producer must also pay the designer's "out of pocket" expenses and transportation to whatever city the production is moved for a try-out.

Finally, the contract calls for payment of the designer's fee in three instalments, one third on the signing of a contract, one third during the rehearsal period, and one third on or before the opening performance.

WHAT ARE THE DESIGNER'S DUTIES?

Answer: The task of a designer in the Broadway theatre is a minute and hectic one. He is responsible for practically everything in the so-called "physical" production.

The immediate task of the scene designer is to supply adequate working drawings or scale models for the carpenter to build from, and color sketches for the painter to paint from. It is not obligatory for the designer to make models for the scenery, since a detailed working drawing, giving all elevations and dimensions, will suffice. When the designer executes a model, it is at his own expense.

The scene designer must also approve all properties, including drapes and furniture, to be used in the production. Usually, he personally will make the bulk of the selections of such properties and visit dozens of stores in the search for the items he thinks the play needs. The stage manager and chief property man on the production usually help the scene designer locate these items. On a big production, the scene designer may run himself ragged "chasing props".

Optional with the producer, the scene designer is also responsible for the designing of special costumes and the supervision of their execution. There is no standard fee for designing costumes. In some cases, the designer may contribute his services on costumes as part of his scene-designing fee. In other cases, he may receive $25 or $50 for each costume sketch, or whatever the traffic will bear.

The designer must supervise the building and painting of his scenery, which is usually executed by contractors. In some cases, one firm builds the scenery and then it is moved to another shop for the paint job. In other cases, a single contractor executes both the building and painting of the scenery.

The scene designer must secure for the producer at

So You Want to Be a Scene Designer? 159

least three bids, or price quotations, from the contractors estimating the cost of building and painting the scenery. From these three bids the producer makes a choice and awards the contract.

In some cases, the scene designer contracts with the producer to deliver the complete scenery for a flat price which includes his designing fee. In this event, the scene designer must be sure that he can get the building and painting done at a price which leaves his fee free and clear.

The scene designer is required to attend the dress rehearsal of the production and to attend the initial out-of-town try-out performance. He must be present to conduct scenic and lighting rehearsals. He must also plot all the necessary lighting and specify the electrical equipment needed for the production.

Occasionally, the producer and the designer agree in advance that a lighting expert will be called in to supervise that part of the production. Ira Ashley and Abe Feder are two Broadway experts who devote themselves to the subject of lighting. However, the union contract expressly gives the designer the right to light a show himself.

In short, from the moment that a scene designer signs a contract for a show, he is "in the trenches". Dress and lighting rehearsals last until all hours of the morning and the spectacle of a bleary-eyed scene designer toying with drapes and squinting at spotlights throughout a nerve-wracking dress rehearsal is a common one in the Broadway theatre.

Not all designers are physically hardy creatures. Often in the Broadway theatre, one finds a wiry, sensitive scene designer patiently struggling with a crew of stage-hands who do not know how to move his scenery about! Stage-hands are not noted for being esthetic folk. Sometimes the most gifted of all scene designers will find himself at a loss to understand why a certain platform fails to move until he discovers that several inches of solid lumber must be planed off!

Finally, dress rehearsals can be terribly expensive, with stage-hands standing around at so much an hour and fumbling their way through an intricate scenic production. The scene designer has to work as swiftly as he knows how, to cut the producer's dress-rehearsal costs; that is, if he wants to remain on good terms with the producer!

Designing a sensitive and imaginative production on paper is one thing. Getting it to work in the practical, hard-boiled theatre is another.

WHAT DOES A SCENE DESIGNER EARN?

Answer: The harsh fact of the matter is that scene designers do not earn very much money in the theatre. In comparison with the ardors of their work already described, the financial returns are ridiculous.

As previously mentioned, the minimum designing fee is $250 for each sketch. In most cases, this also happens

So You Want to Be a Scene Designer? 161

to be the maximum. A designer of average reputation who receives over $1,000 for designing and supervising a three-set production is doing well in the Broadway scheme of things. For a one-set show, $500, or perhaps $750, is a good price, although many designers do a one-set show for the absolute minimum of $250. A designer who earns a fee of $2,500 for a one-set show is the most expensive man in the business.

It is also a sad fact in the theatre that while the union contract provides that the scene designer be paid for his work by the producer in three instalments, too often the scene designer never receives his last payment! As a result, most designers try to jack up their price and figure on the first two instalments as full payment, the last instalment becoming "gravy".

Now, examine the fact that there are approximately 120 new dramatic productions on Broadway each season and perhaps an additional 10 musical comedies and revues. There are approximately 60 active scene designers who are members of the union. That would give each designer about two productions a season to design, if they were equally divided.

But there is no such equal distribution of the work. One designer may perform his services for as many as a dozen productions each season, while another may not even do one. The man who has done a dozen productions in a single Broadway season has worked frantically.

Jo Mielziner during recent Broadway seasons has been very much in demand among the producers and has designed production after production. Yet Mielziner's gross earnings for his Broadway designing in a single season are not much above $20,000. When you earn that kind of money you are on the very top as a Broadway designer. Very few designers come anywhere near it.

The average earning power of most successful Broadway designers is between $5,000 and $8,000 a season, hardly a princely income in the theatre. To earn that much, you must be established and in favor.

On the other hand, most scene designers are hard pressed to earn a bare living in the theatre. The problem of the struggling designer who is trying to keep alive is one that has brought another difficult condition in the theatre, one that the union has not been able to cope with altogether.

A designer who is anxious to earn at least something, and to keep his name prominent, will frequently cut his price secretly. It's open knowledge along Broadway that some designers will sign the regular union contract with a producer and then "kick back" part of the fee, so that he is working for a fee below the minimum scale. This condition doesn't militate for increasing the general earning power of scene designers as a class.

If you think you can become rich by designing the

So You Want to Be a Scene Designer? 163

scenery for Broadway plays, you're blowing soap bubbles. It's a hard, rocky, and tortuous road and you won't make a fortune out of it, no matter how famous you become.

WHAT ARE A SCENE DESIGNER'S EXPENSES?

Answer: If the foregoing has seemed slightly harrowing, add to your shock the fact that out of the fee the designer receives from the producer, he must also deduct various expenses that are inevitably incurred in doing a show.

Most designers have the expense of maintaining some kind of a studio. Rent and telephone are both involved.

There are also the expenses of materials which a designer must use in designing a play, instruments, paper, inks, water colors, models, drawing boards, etc.

A designer who is at all active in the theatre finds it impossible to do all the work without an assistant. He must pay the assistant's salary out of his own pocket.

Add such items as cab-fares while rushing about town covering all the details on a production, tips, phone calls, lunches, etc.

It all adds up to a total expense that knocks a considerable figure off a designer's earnings, perhaps as high as 25%.

CAN A SCENE DESIGNER PAINT HIS OWN SCENERY?

Answer: Yes.

If you are a member of the United Scenic Artists, you can either design or paint scenery or both. As a result, there are some occasions when a designer will contract to design a show for a producer at the minimum fee because he also counts on doing the paint job himself and earning some additional money.

But the other members of the union, who confine themselves to painting scenery, don't like it too much, since it keeps them out of work. A scene designer who consistently paints his own scenery will have pressure brought to bear on him by his fellow union members.

CAN A SCENE DESIGNER BUILD HIS OWN SCENERY?

Answer: No.

Scenery can only be built by members of the famous "Local Number One", the union to which only stagehands may belong.

The scene designer who is so intrepid as to pick up a hammer and drive a nail into a piece of scenery will quickly incur the wrath of the carpenters.

The various brotherhoods of the theatre are friendly associations, but they do not take liberties with each other.

So, if you have devoted years of studying how to build scenery somewhere, it won't mean much to you on Broadway, except that you will be able to supervise such work as a designer.

HOW DOES THE DESIGNER WORK WITH THE DIRECTOR?

Answer: They work hand in hand.

Before a designer proceeds to design the scenery for a play, he has an extended conference with the director in which they come to an agreement on what the scenery should include. The director must plot all his "business" and stage positions, including entrances and exits, in terms of the finished scenery.

Since, during the major portion of the rehearsal period, the director rehearses his company on a bare stage, he must have a specific idea of what the scenery will be like. Furthermore, he may have definite notions as to the mood of the play in connection with the style of his direction, which should be complemented by the scenery and lighting.

As a result, before the director can begin rehearsing properly, he must receive from the designer a detailed floor plan of the scenery, usually a blue print. From this floor plan, the stage manager will mark in chalk on the rehearsal stage the outlines of each set, indicating all entrances, windows, stair-cases, landings, positions of furniture, etc.

The conference between the designer and director is of extreme importance. Once they have come to a complete decision together, the results are final. The only way to make changes later is to build new scenery!

Frequently, directors have expressed surprise when confronted with the actual scenery for a play at the first dress rehearsal. Perhaps they have not understood what the designer meant when they first discussed the scenery, or perhaps the designer did not make himself too clear.

It's always advisable for a designer to be absolutely sure that the director is intimately aware of every detail on the blue print, before the scenery goes into construction.

WHAT DOES DESIGNING IN THE THEATRE LEAD TO?

Answer: If you confine yourself to designing in the Broadway theatre, your future and financial independence is limited.

However, once a designer has won a reputation in the Broadway theatre, there are many other ways for him to make a great deal of money.

A number of successful Broadway stage designers have reaped a harvest in the field of commercial designing. Henry Dreyfuss and Norman Bel Geddes are two who have been paid fancy prices for creating the designs of refrigerators, locomotives, lamps, furniture, offices, banks, etc. The trend in commercial design is modern, and stream-line effects have become very popular. Many Broadway designers who have brought a smart, modern dècor into their stage settings, have

So You Want to Be a Scene Designer? 167

been called upon to do a great deal of commercial work.

There is also an opportunity for Broadway stage designers to work for the opera. Robert Edmond Jones, Jo Mielziner, Donald Oenslager, Urban, Jorgulesco, and others have been given commissions by the Metropolitan Opera Company and musical organizations in other cities.

There are also opportunities for well-known Broadway designers to work in fairly closely allied fields. Jones, Albert Johnson, Boris Aronson, Vincent Minelli, and others have designed settings for motion picture houses which give stage presentations in addition to showing pictures, such as the Rockefeller Center Music Hall, "Roxy's", etc.

Also, several Broadway stage designers have been engaged by motion picture companies, both in New York and in Hollywood. Robert Edmond Jones, for instance, has been very active in designing scenery and costumes for motion pictures that have been made in Technicolor.

Some designers do private interior decorating for additional revenue to supplement their theatre earnings.

Finally, there is nothing to prevent a scene designer from becoming a producer. Norman Bel Geddes and Jo Mielziner are among those who have become managers; Bel Geddes, in particular, is the producer of Sidney Kingsley's enormously successful "Dead End".

There *is* a future for a stage designer. But, if you examine the foregoing closely, you will discover that there is no real reason why one must begin as a designer in the theatre to enter any of these other fields, except that winning a reputation helps. However, one can start from scratch as an interior decorator or commercial designer, for instance, and perhaps eventually win a reputation without having been in the theatre.

SECTION VI

SO YOU WANT TO BE A STAGE MANAGER?

"It is characteristic of the run-of-the-mine theatrical producer that in his selection of so important a factor in the successful opening and operating of his play as the stage manager, the criteria he brings to bear in making his selection are invariably as haphazard and witless as those he applied to his choice of the play in the first place. He picks him because the stage manager has hung about the office in the early stage of production making himself useful to the point where the producer is beholden to him; because, knowing the prospective stage manager's economic situation, he can calculate to underpay him for valuable service by taking advantage of that knowledge; because, since the job is simply a job in a field where any job is precious, the producer can hand it out in a lord-of-the-manor manner and catch for himself the fine feeling one gets from distributing largesse; because, being by background, training and culture, the sort of person who would think of Gordon Craig as a brand of Scotch whiskey, he minimizes the importance of the stage manager, looking upon him as 'the guy who holds the book and runs the curtain up and down' when, in reality, it is only through able stage managing that a perfect fusion of play and performance is obtained."

— EARL MCGILL, *famous Broadway stage manager, to the author*

SO YOU WANT TO BE A STAGE MANAGER?
Answer: Well, it's not the most exalted position in the theatre, but it's a position of responsibility and authority.

Many people have started in the theatre as stage managers to get experience and have gone on to become directors and producers. Particularly during the rehearsal stages of a production, stage managing is hard and nerve-wracking work, requiring constant alertness in the most trying circumstances.

A really good stage manager is a great asset to a production. Furthermore, a crack stage manager is always appreciated in the theatre, by producers, directors, actors, stage-hands, and company managers.

If you want to learn things in the theatre, it's a good idea to start off as a stage manager.

WHAT DOES A STAGE MANAGER DO?
Answer: He is general utility assistant to the director.

From the day that he is engaged for the production, he begins plotting on paper the thousand and one details that he will have to execute during the rehearsal period. These duties include gathering up the properties and special effects that the play requires during rehearsal, drawing a plot of the electrical equipment that he is told by the designer will be needed, consulting with the chief electrician, chief carpenter, and chief property man on what will be required for the show, etc.

During the rehearsal period he will hold the prompt-manuscript and make careful notations of every instruction or piece of direction given to the cast by the director.

When rehearsals begin, the stage manager usually sits at a table on one side of the stage with his prompt-script before him. As soon as the actors have learned their lines and put their parts aside, the stage manager must watch the dialogue of the play like a hawk and prompt any actors in the cast who stumble through their lines. This kind of prompting, however, is extremely tricky, for sometimes the actor may be figuring out a piece of "business" and does not want to be prompted. It's a real knack for a stage manager to sense when the actor not only needs but also wants prompting.

He will also note carefully in the prompt-script every change of dialogue made by the playwright during rehearsal and keep the manuscript up to date from one day of rehearsal to the next. Sometimes, a manuscript goes through so many changes and cuts in a single day of rehearsal that a stage manager may have to sit up all night typing all the corrections so that

So You Want to Be a Stage Manager?

his manuscript is clean and legible for the next morning at rehearsal.

There are humorous legends in the theatre concerning stage managers who deliberately have kept their prompt-manuscripts in such condition that they alone could translate it, in order to be sure of their jobs! A conscientious stage manager, however, is proud of having a clean-looking prompt-script. Some stage managers even go to elaborate pains with the "book", as the prompt-script is often called. All stage-business will be marked in colored ink or pencil, and warnings for effects, entrances, and lighting cues will be scored on the side of the dialogue in impressive fashion. The prompt-script is very important. Often, the director, who has created a piece of "business", may not remember what it was he suggested to the actor and must refer to the "book" to refresh his memory.

The prompt-script, or a copy of it, is used by publishing houses when plays are published.

It is the only complete record of what has been done to a play during the rehearsal period.

The stage manager is custodian of the prompt-script.

Throughout the entire rehearsal period, the stage manager acts as a kind of secretary for the director and makes notations of everything the director thinks is necessary for the production from one day to the next. The stage manager also is responsible for purchasing and assembling many of the hand properties and special effects.

After the play has opened, the stage manager is in sole charge of discipline backstage, supervising both the cast and the crew of stage-hands. There are some stage managers who "boss" the crew during the dress rehearsal period, but this is not always necessary. A good crew will resent interference from a stage manager, unless they know him and respect him. Incidentally, a good crew is invaluable to a stage manager and can help him enormously.

During the run of the play, the stage manager is responsible for ringing up the curtain on time and usually keeps a record each night of the running time of the performance. This is done to determine when the cast is playing the show too fast or perhaps slowing it up. It is his express duty to see that the cast assembles in the dressing rooms well before curtain time.

He must stand in the wings at all times and "hold the book" as a prompter, unless he assigns this duty to his assistant. Most stage managers are reluctant to surrender this duty, however.

The stage-manager "warns" the electrician and property man on all light cues and special effects and gives the orders for them to be executed on cue.

He also must be sure that the members of the cast are "warned" when they are due on stage and to be

So You Want to Be a Stage Manager? 175

sure that they are in the wings ready to make their entrances.

During the entire engagement of the play, the stage manager serves as the producer's representative. He should report to the producer's office daily and inform the producer of any difficulties he may be experiencing with the cast or crew, if such occur.

Another important duty of the stage manager is to conduct and supervise regular understudy rehearsals and to be sure that all actors engaged to understudy are on hand and adequately rehearsed to jump in and give a performance in the event of emergency. Usually, understudy rehearsals are conducted once a week, but the stage manager may call as many understudy rehearsals as he deems necessary.

In some cases, the stage manager directs "second" productions, particularly when the director of the play is not available. The producer of a successful Broadway play may decide to send several companies on the road, or he may even send a company to London. On these occasions, the stage manager is sometimes called upon to direct the "second" company, since he is familiar with all of the original stage-business created by the director. Almost invariably, he does a carbon-copy job, following his prompt-script literally, unless he happens to have some new ideas that are approved by the producer.

It's plain to see that stage managing is a man-sized job.

HOW DO YOU GET A JOB AS A STAGE MANAGER?

Answer: Very much the way an actor gets a job, by "going the rounds" and inquiring of producers if they intend doing a show and whether they need a stage manager.

If you happen to be ambitious as a director and can interest a producer in you in that respect, you may be able to persuade him to give you a chance at stage-managing, should he be reluctant to engage you as a director. The point is that a man who seems to have some background or talent as a director may very reasonably be an excellent stage manager.

Some stars insist on having a stage manager with whom they are familiar.

Another method of getting a job as a stage manager is to attach yourself to a director.

DO MOST DIRECTORS "CARRY" THEIR OWN STAGE MANAGERS?

Answer: There are some directors who will not do a show unless their own stage manager is on the production. Directors rely heavily on good stage managers for the execution of details.

Almost all directors have several men around whom they value as stage managers.

But, of course, some directors may stage more than

So You Want to Be a Stage Manager?

one play a season, or, again, the stage manager they want may not be available. However, a director who is familiar with the work of a stage manager is often instrumental in getting that man a job. Most producers allow a director to engage his own stage manager, unless the producer happens to have a stage manager on his permanent staff.

WHAT SALARY DOES A STAGE MANAGER EARN?

Answer: A crackerjack stage manager may earn $150 a week, although a salary that high is rare along Broadway.

The average salary paid to a competent stage manager is about $100 a week, although salaries for experienced men range as low as $50 and $75 a week.

IS A STAGE MANAGER PAID DURING THE REHEARSAL PERIOD?

Answer: This is entirely at the disposition of the producer.

In some cases the stage manager is paid half-salary during each week of rehearsals, in other cases he is not paid during rehearsals at all.

DOES A STAGE MANAGER HAVE TO BE AN ACTOR?

Answer: You don't have to be a talented actor, but you should have some ability.

Many stage managers are required to play small parts in addition to stage managing. Usually, when a stage manager plays a part, he has an assistant stage manager to take over his duties while he is on stage.

DO STAGE MANAGERS HAVE A UNION?

Answer: No, but they all must belong to Actors' Equity which gives them the same protection it provides for its actors.

The stage manager signs a regular Equity contract with the producer, which guarantees him two weeks of bonded salary. He is subject to all the rules and regulations of Equity of which he is a full member.

As a result of this representation, stage managers do not need a union of their own.

WHAT TECHNICAL KNOWLEDGE MUST A STAGE MANAGER POSSESS?

Answer: Not a great deal.

That is, a stage manager does not have to know how to operate a portable switch board, or how to set up scenery, or any of the purely technical details of the theatre.

The stage-hands are highly organized and no one may take over their actual work. All a stage manager need supervise technically on a production are the general elements, such as the fact that the scenery must be set up in a reasonable amount of time and that the lighting be executed on cue, etc.

A shrewd stage manager does not interfere with his crew. If he thinks any member of his crew is incompetent, he informs the producer and a new man is obtained after the producer files a complaint with the union.

Of course, if a stage manager happens to be a technical expert, it is distinctly to his advantage, since he can detect incompetence quickly. But it is not obligatory.

A quick-witted stage manager can pick up most of the necessary technical information he needs after having worked on one or two productions as an assistant. Most of his duties depend on his general intelligence and personality.

HOW MANY JOBS ARE THERE FOR STAGE MANAGERS?

Answer: Every production must have a stage manager and some productions may carry one or more assistant stage managers.

Since there are approximately one hundred and twenty legitimate stage productions during each Broadway season, it follows that there are approximately one hundred and twenty jobs open for stage managers and perhaps half that number for assistants.

Of course, just as in the case of an actor who appears in more than one play a season, reducing the total number of jobs available to actors, some stage managers are employed in more than one production a season, so that the figure of approximately one hundred and twenty stage managing jobs available each season may be reduced to about one hundred opportunities.

HOW MANY STAGE MANAGERS ARE THERE ON BROADWAY?

Answer: This is difficult to calculate exactly, but certainly each Broadway producer has at least one stage manager on his list who has worked for him on a production.

Also, many actors are potentially stage managers or have had experience as such and, when unable to obtain an acting engagement, will seek a stage managing job.

Again, there are many former stock-company directors who, finding stock work a thing of the past, seek stage managing positions on Broadway.

It is probably no exaggeration to state that there are five hundred people looking for work as stage managers each season on Broadway.

DO PRODUCERS EMPLOY STAGE MANAGERS UNDER LONG-TERM CONTRACT?

Answer: Only on very few occasions, and even on those, a written contract is seldom in existence.

Some producers will support their staff stage managers during periods when they are not producing, to be sure that they are available when needed and not working for another producer. But only very powerful and rich producers will do this.

What usually happens during slack periods, is that a stage manager who has worked for a producer on a production will sit around the producer's office and

So You Want to Be a Stage Manager?

do general office work for nothing until the producer gets busy.

WHAT IS THE FUTURE IN STAGE MANAGING?
Answer: It is a very definite stepping stone to directing.

There are some stage managers who never advance, but who continue in the theatre for many years at the same work. A top-notch stage manager, once he is established, usually manages to keep working, unless he has bad luck through becoming attached to productions that are failures.

For all-around practical experience, however, stage managing should be prescribed for everyone in the theatre who wants to become either a director or a producer.

It's baptism by fire.

SECTION VII

SO YOU WANT TO BE A COMPANY MANAGER OR A PRESS AGENT?

"Somehow it is impossible for me to mention the profession of the Legitimate Theatre Press Representative without smiling. Perhaps the humor is in that word 'Representative'. It used to be 'Agent'. He was the guy with the free ducats who drank with the newspaper boys. But we are a dignified lot today. Ever so dignified. Of course, we still get drunk. But only sometimes with the newspaper boys. And even when we do we are apt not to mention the show we are 'representing'. If I know what I'm talking about (because no two press representatives are prone to agree on anything) Ethics have crept into our peculiar midst. Our ways may be devious, but our facts are authenticated. We can do some pretty helpful things for a hit, or just a good show. But I think we are as helpless as ushers in an empty theatre when it comes to a show the public does not choose to like."

> — BEN WASHER, *former drama columnist for the* N. Y. World-Telegram *and now a leading Broadway press agent, in a letter to the author*

SO YOU WANT TO BE A COMPANY MANAGER OR A PRESS AGENT?

Answer: While these are two separate jobs in the theatre, on many occasions you may be called on to "double in brass", which means you do both.

When a play goes on tour, a company manager and a press agent invariably visit each "stand" before the production arrives, to arrange all details. This is known as "advance" work. Some producers will send out only one advance man to take care of all publicity and business arrangements.

Of the two jobs, the work of the press agent is more of a creative nature and generally more important to the life of a production than that of a company manager. However, especially on tour, a good company manager is a very necessary employee.

Press agentry along Broadway is practically a fine art. Doing the work of a company manager consists partially of doing what any good accountant can do, plus possessing native shrewdness as a business-man and "knowing the ropes" in the theatre.

WHAT ARE A COMPANY MANAGER'S DUTIES?

Answer: If the producer has a general manager in his employ, the duties of a company manager are confined to the business of the company he is managing. But, in most cases, the producer has no general manager and the company manager handles all the business of the production from the beginning of rehearsals on through the run of the play until after it closes.

In this case, it is the company manager's task to handle all the business arrangements and details that come up through the production and operating of a play, referring to the producer on final commitments and payments. During the rehearsal period, the responsibilities of the company manager are not great if the producer himself handles the business. He is usually responsible for obtaining in advance any licenses which may be necessary during the run of the play, such as gun permits, theatre licenses, etc.

Once the play opens, the job of the company manager begins in earnest. If the play is sent out of town for a try-out before coming to New York, the company manager must attend to all the details of moving the production and cast, baggage transfer, hotel accommodations, etc.

The company manager is in the theatre box-office before curtain time at each performance and gauges the ticket sale. When it looks as though there will be a weak audience, he arranges for "papering the house", if he thinks it advisable. This will mean distributing passes to people whose attendance he believes will

So You Want to Be a Company Manager? 187

make for valuable word-of-mouth publicity. A good company manager is sparing with passes, since the "dead beat" is hated in the theatre.

After the curtain has gone up on each performance and the sale of seats is closed, the company manager proceeds to "count the house". He checks carefully each unsold ticket left on the rack, which is called "dead wood", and compares the total with the stubs of all the tickets which have been sold. These stubs are removed from the ticket-taker's box and counted. Entries are made on a trial box-office statement. Finally, the disposition of all passes is entered. When the trial statement, called "the rough", is completed and all the figures tally with the gross number of tickets which were originally on the rack, he proceeds to make up his final statement for the performance. Usually a dozen carbon copies are made, since individual copies must be forwarded to the producer, playwright, investors, etc. All copies of the box-office statements are signed by the company manager and co-signed by the box-office treasurer and theatre manager as correct.

When the statement is completed, the box-office treasurer turns over to the company manager whatever cash the producer of the play is entitled to on the performance. This cash is deposited by the company manager to the producer's account. In some theatres, all receipts are collected by the theatre owner and a check for the amount due is either given to the company manager or forwarded direct to the producer.

At the end of the week, the company manager must make up a statement for the entire week, listing all the gross receipts and expenses of the production. On this statement he enters the weekly profit or loss that the production has shown.

The company manager is responsible for all cash disbursements made from the box-office for the company. No cash may be paid out from the box-office without his written okay. Such items include advances in salary to the cast or crew, C.O.D.'s delivered to the box-office, purchase of railroad tickets, etc.

The company manager almost always handles the payroll and pays the weekly salaries due to all members of the company, except in cases when the producer prefers to pay by check.

Pay-day is usually on Saturday afternoon, during the matinée performance. The company manager makes up the payroll and gives each member of the company his salary, in each case receiving signatures acknowledging payment in full on his payroll sheet. From each salary, he deducts all advances in salary that may have been granted during the week and charges for tickets to the play that may have been ordered by members of the company. Whenever advances in salary are granted by the company manager, or whenever tickets have been ordered by members of the company, he

So You Want to Be a Company Manager?
always demands a receipt. These receipts are returned in the pay envelopes when deductions are made.

Another duty sometimes imposed on the company manager is to see that the star or featured members of a company are kept satisfied. This entails going backstage at least once during a performance to inquire whether anything may be wanted. In some cases, the company manager brings a box-office statement for each performance backstage for the star to examine, particularly when the star is working for a percentage of the gross receipts.

The company manager always keeps in touch with the producer's office, especially if the play is on tour. In the latter case, he wires or telephones the producer after each performance or whenever he deems it advisable.

When a company manager discovers at the end of the week that he does not have enough cash on hand to pay the salaries, he communicates with the producer. Usually, the company manager can tell pretty much a day or two in advance how things will stand by Saturday. There are legends about company managers who upon wiring the home office for funds have received no reply. That's when a company manager has to use his ingenuity!

WHAT DOES A COMPANY MANAGER EARN?
Answer: If he happens to be general manager for the producer and everything is rosy with the show, he may

get as high as $200 a week, but a good company manager who earns $150 a week considers himself well paid.

Most company managers receive $100 a week, or less.

Company managers often attach themselves to a producing office in the hope of becoming general manager.

WHAT ARE THE DUTIES OF A PRESS AGENT? *Answer:* To get publicity for the show through every possible medium, including newspapers, news reels, radio, billboards, posters, streamers, sandwich men in all their variations, and by word of mouth, etc.

Many impressive books have been written on the methods and devices of obtaining publicity and in the theatre there are a host of stories and anecdotes told about famous publicity stunts. Plays have been "made" by publicity, plays have been ruined by publicity. Sometimes publicity comes when the press agent least expects it. Sometimes he is delighted by unlooked-for publicity "breaks", sometimes he is filled with disgust by them.

Theatrical publicity is one of the more rarefied forms of all publicity, a field unique to itself.

Along Broadway, the press agent is concerned not only with getting space in the New York papers, but with "breaking" stories that hit the press of the nation, since a large part of the Broadway theatre audi-

So You Want to Be a Company Manager? 191

ence consists of visitors from other cities. The fame of a play must spread for it to do business. Generally, however, the Broadway press agent trains his guns on the New York papers, since he can count on out-of-town papers "picking up" his stuff when the news is important or interesting. Also, there are syndicate services, such as the Associated Press and United Press which forward daily information throughout the country.

From the day that he is engaged by the producer, usually during the rehearsal period, the press agent begins writing various feature stories about the play, the actors, the author, the producer, things that happen during rehearsal, how the scenery works if the production is elaborate, and every item he can think of, or discover, that he hopes will be interesting enough to get in print and that will make people want to see the play.

He next attempts to "plant" these stories with newspapers, either on the drama pages or in the news columns.

He also sends out regular releases announcing the opening of the play, the names of the cast and director, the theatre at which it will be played, etc. These releases are sent to all drama editors, both in New York and suburban.

At the top of each release he puts his name, address and phone number and a suggested release date.

These regular releases are either mailed to the newspapers or delivered by messenger.

It is the duty of the press agent to arrange for everyone of importance in the cast either to be photographed at the expense of the producer or else to submit their own photographs. These photographs are used both for newspaper reproduction and for lobby displays. The press agent also arranges for drawings to be made of the cast and placed in newspapers, whenever possible, trying to get these drawings from free lance artists for nothing.

The press agent usually composes all advertising copy, an important task. A good paid advertising campaign can be very helpful to a show. He usually recommends to the producer those newspapers and periodicals where he thinks advertising will be valuable.

The press agent also is responsible for the "press list", which is made up by him each day and delivered to the box-office several hours before curtain time. This "press list" consists of passes given by the press agent to members of the fourth estate or to people from whom he thinks he can get publicity for the play. The press agent is usually sparing with his press list and gives tickets out grudgingly. In some cases, the list is limited by the producer, particularly when the play is a success.

The press agent's major press lists are the two he

So You Want to Be a Company Manager? makes up for the opening night and second night performance. On these two lists he includes all the important drama critics. He is responsible for forwarding these tickets to the critics and must be sure that no one has been ignored. Opening night, particularly, is all-important, and he must be certain that he sends good locations to the critics, most of whom prefer to sit "on the aisle".

After the play has opened, the press agent, in addition to his other efforts to get publicity, will seek out organizations and societies. He will prepare brochures, handbills, etc., designed to catch the attention of the general public. He will try to arrange for some of the actors in the cast to make radio appearances and always be on the lookout for a good interview that will get into print.

He will seek all kinds of "tie-ups" and "stunts" that will bring the show free publicity, such as arranging for members of the cast to pose for fashion-pictures, etc.

Any publicity medium that meets the public eye will be a fair target for his efforts, if it can help the show.

WHAT MAKES A "GOOD" PRESS AGENT?

Answer: There are several general factors, including the ability to write lively stories and copy, native ingenuity and the knack of capitalizing on news events that can be "tied in" with the show, aggressiveness, charm of manner and approach, a lively imagination, etc.

All of these, however, are secondary to knowing the gentlemen of the press intimately and to having good publicity connections.

Newspapermen, particularly city editors, are chary of publicity stunts. An ordinary publicity release coming through the mails from an unknown press agent usually winds up in the waste-basket. Newspaper editors do not want to print "phony" stories. If they do not know the author of the publicity, they are prone to disregard it unless they can check its authenticity.

A good press agent must know his customers intimately. He sells his stuff principally to the newspapers. Consequently, he must be familiar with newspapermen personally and know their preferences. "I think so-and-so will come up for this one," a good press agent will mutter to himself on cooking up a publicity yarn, meaning he knows that a certain editor will like the story and print it.

Newspaper editors have been "burned" so frequently by fantastic stories they have printed about the theatre, that a Broadway press agent has to know his way about with them thoroughly in order to get any space.

Naturally, he concentrates on the drama editors and critics and gets to know them all personally. In addition, he must develop "ins" with feature writers, syndi-

So You Want to Be a Company Manager?
cate writers, city editors, managing editors, etc. Not until he has established himself with all these hard-boiled fry as being reliable and colorful, can a press agent hope to be really "good".

Another factor in being a "good" publicity man is getting free publicity that *helps* the show. There is an adage in the theatre which runs, "All publicity is good publicity except bad publicity."

Frequently, a press agent will be doing his best work for a show when he manages to keep a story *out* of the papers. That's where "connections" are invaluable.

A "good" publicity man must spend a great deal of time consorting with newspapermen. As far as a press agent is concerned, a newspaper man can do no wrong.

WHAT DOES A PRESS AGENT EARN?
Answer: As high as $200 a week, particularly if you are handling a lavish production. The average salary for a press agent is $100 a week, scaling down as low as $50.

However, a "good" press agent may handle several shows at one time and make as much as $500 a week that way. Some producers prefer their press agent to work exclusively for them, but usually he is free to handle other productions.

HOW DOES A PRESS AGENT GET A JOB?
Answer: Either by knowing a producer personally or by being recommended for the job.

It so happens that there is a charmed inner circle among the Broadway press agents. There are approximately a dozen men and women all told who do the bulk of the work each season. Newspapermen are indifferent to newcomers and prefer to rely on the efforts of the press agents they already know and like. As a result, a producer will seldom entrust the job of publicity on a show to someone who is not already thoroughly experienced and established on Broadway.

In fact, most producers swear by the press agents who have worked for them for many years and will not make a change under any circumstances.

However, if you are energetic and show signs of general intelligence and imagination, you can sometimes walk in on a producer and persuade him to give you a chance.

WHO ARE THE BEST-KNOWN BROADWAY PRESS AGENTS?

Answer: Among those who are well established and work regularly as press agents for the Broadway producers are Richard Maney, Charles Washburn, Arthur Levy, Bernard Sobel, Ben Washer, Nat Dorfman, Joe Heydt, Phyllis Pearlman, Helen Deutsch, Bernard Simon, John Peter Toohey, Dave Lipsky, Jim Proctor, Mollie Steinberg, Max Gendel and Theodore Goldsmith.

Claude Greneker supervises all press activities for

So You Want to Be a Company Manager? 197

the Messrs. Shubert and Russell Crouse performs a similar service for the Theatre Guild.

WHAT EXPERIENCE DO YOU NEED TO BECOME A PRESS AGENT?

Answer: Many press agents have started out by working for a newspaper, which is commonly considered the best of all possible backgrounds for a press agent.

However, if you have any reputation as an author, either through having sold stories or articles to magazines, or through having had a book published, you will be viewed with a certain favor as a potential press agent.

Sometimes, working for an advertising office is considered good experience. Practical experience can also be obtained by starting as an assistant to an established press agent. "Zolotow's Guide" contains a complete list of all active press agents and where they can be located.

Finally, you don't need any experience at all to become a press agent, if you feel you have a general aptitude for thinking up ideas that will get into print. It's considerably more difficult to get a job on this premise.

WHAT EXPERIENCE DO YOU NEED TO BECOME A COMPANY MANAGER?

Answer: You have to know all the business of the theatre. The only way to acquire this is to work in the Broadway theatre.

Many company managers have begun with producers as office boys. Others have been actors or cloak-room attendants. Stage managers have become company managers. Ushers have become company managers. Door men have become company managers.

But it's just about impossible to get a job as a company manager unless you know the Broadway theatre at first hand.

WHAT DOES COMPANY MANAGING OR PRESS AGENTRY LEAD TO?

Answer: You can make a good living, for one thing, particularly if you become a successful press agent.

Your jobs are entirely dependent on working for a producer whose play is a success, however, and you can have good luck and bad. But if you're working on a successful play, or two, it's an easy and congenial way to earn a handsome living. You can usually save enough out of your earnings, if you have a good season, to enjoy a pleasant summer vacation.

Many press agents have been engaged by motion picture companies as publicity men and as writers.

On the other hand, many company managers and press agents have forged ahead in the theatre as producers. Also, many press agents have become playwrights. Jed Harris, Herman Shumlin, S. N. Behrman, Arthur Hopkins, Theron Bamberger, Irving Cooper, Alex Yokel, Patterson McNutt, William Brady, Morris Gest, Sam Grisman, George Haight, Thomas Kil-

So You Want to Be a Company Manager?

patrick, Forrest Haring and many others began in the theatre as press agents or company managers.

Finally, both are jobs in the theatre which depend on your executive abilities and resourcefulness. You can count on having a lively time in the theatre, if you are either a company manager or a press agent. And, if you are both at the same time, you'll have to move fast!

SECTION VIII

SO YOU WANT TO BE A DRAMA CRITIC?

"If you can devote just one chapter to convincing the Mantle correspondents that I know of no possible easy road to becoming a drama critic, your book will be worth a lot both to me and **a** number of other fellows."

— BURNS MANTLE, *in a letter to the author*

SO YOU WANT TO BE A DRAMA CRITIC?

Answer: Practically everyone who goes to see a play finds himself in the position of being a critic. If you see a play or a performance, you form some sort of an opinion about what you have seen; that is, either you like it or you do not.

No one can dispute your right to an opinion in the theatre. Your opinion is just as good as the next fellow's. The fact that he doesn't happen to agree with you will not rob you of your personal convictions. But your ability as a critic depends largely on how well you are able to articulate your opinions.

When you come right down to it, the only difference between you and a professional critic is that he happens to be paid for it and has the added advantage of being able to put his opinions into print. He is paid because the public wants to read his opinions. Frequently, many of us who do not enjoy this privilege would like to assume the position of those who do. It so happens that the opportunity does not usually present itself, since the writing of drama criticism is a restricted field, as you shall see.

The metropolitan drama critics have been assailed time and again, publicly and privately, by those who do not agree with them. The point to remember is that, in the final analysis, any form of criticism in the theatre, printed or verbal, privately expressed or publicly, must be personal and founded on an individual person's analysis, general erudition, taste, and perception.

The professional critics of the theatre are only human. They either like or dislike a play, a performance, a set of scenery, or a production, say so, and explain why. If you don't happen to agree with them, they can't help it. They can only render as criticism what they believe to be the truth as they see it.

No critic can do any more.

WHERE CAN YOU GET A JOB AS A DRAMA CRITIC?

Answer: Before really probing this question, let us first examine the situation in New York and dispose of that.

There is no disputing the fact that the professional theatre is centered in New York. As a result, the major posts for drama critics exist on the metropolitan daily papers in that city. There are a few important newspapers outside of New York, such as the Boston *Transcript* and the Baltimore *Sun,* whose drama critics have been able to wield some national influence, but, by and large, the only critics who exert any real and immediate influence on the theatre are those who review the plays in New York.

So You Want to Be a Drama Critic?

About the only sure way for a newcomer to become a drama critic on a New York newspaper is to buy the newspaper.

There are only ten important daily newspapers in New York, all told. The *American, Brooklyn Eagle, Daily Mirror, Daily News, Evening Journal, Evening Post, Herald-Tribune, Times, Sun,* and the *World-Telegram*.

Each of these newspapers is a powerful commercial institution, designed to make money for its publisher.

As a result, no newspaper published in New York will pay money to a drama critic who does not enjoy prestige, authority and a measure of public acceptance. Furthermore, New York critics have held their positions over a period of many years and even their assistants are hand-picked. Only on very rare occasions does a New York drama critic quit his job.

The simple truth of the matter is that there are no openings in New York and on those solemn occasions when they do exist the publisher looks about for someone with a "name" and a reputation.

You might as well resign yourself to the fact that there is no way for you to "break in" as a drama critic on a major New York newspaper.

WHAT OTHER OPPORTUNITIES ARE THERE FOR DRAMA CRITICS?

Answer: There are several publications devoted wholly or in part to the theatre, including *Stage, Variety,*

Billboard, Theatre Arts Monthly, New Theatre, etc. Here again, very few openings exist and when they do, the publishers of these periodicals invariably fill the positions with already established critics.

There are a number of "class" magazines, which maintain theatre sections, such as *Vogue, Esquire,* the *New Yorker, Life, Judge,* the *Nation,* the *New Republic,* etc. All of these are national publications and employ as drama critics those who are established and command a following.

There are a host of lesser publications, with small circulations, that employ drama critics. These little publications come and pass from the scene each year. If you are glib and have any background at all, sometimes you can convince the publisher of one of these magazines to give you a chance reviewing plays, probably at a nominal salary, or, worse yet, at no salary at all.

(A full list of such publications can be found in the annual special edition of Editor and Publisher, or by writing to the publishers of that trade magazine, which makes its offices in the Times Building, New York. The N. W. Ayer Advertising Agency, 500 Fifth Avenue, New York, also publishes an annual list of publications in the United States.)

Drama critics of these obscure magazines command almost no prestige, since they have only a tiny reading audience. As a matter of fact, most Broadway press agents usually have never even heard of many of these publications and will send press-tickets to their drama critics only upon written request, and, at that, reluctantly. If you are reviewing plays for an obscure publication and find yourself on the press agent's "second night" list, count yourself lucky.

About the only other field where you can seek a job as a drama critic exists outside of New York. The key cities, such as Boston, Philadelphia, Washington, Chicago, Pittsburgh, all have large newspapers which employ drama critics. But the days of the road in the theatre have long since seen their peak and comparatively few Broadway productions go on tour. Also many newspapers outside of New York buy syndicated features about the theatre on space.

What usually happens on most newspapers outside of New York is that one man is assigned to covering several departments, usually with the emphasis laid on motion picture criticism, supplemented by an occasional job of reviewing a play that happens to be in town. On some of these newspapers, one critic will "cover" radio, motion pictures, the theatre, and perhaps write a piece on important musical events, as well.

In short, with very few exceptions, drama criticism on the newspapers outside of New York is not regarded as very important. And that brings you back to New York where there are no jobs open for drama critics!

WHAT IS THE BEST KIND OF EXPERIENCE TO BECOME A DRAMA CRITIC?

Answer: Dismissing the New York scene and confining the question to the papers outside of that city, the best way to become a drama critic is to start as a newspaperman. Very few publishers will let you start out as a critic. You have to work your way up from the city room. You may start as a reporter, or, if you're lucky, as a feature writer with a "by-line." You may also start on a desk job as a re-write man or perhaps as an assistant editor.

There's a general feeling around newspapers that a newspaperman is one who works in his shirt-sleeves, whereas a critic is a chap who carries a cane.

As a result, before you can become a critic on most papers, you must first serve your apprenticeship as a newspaperman. Just walking in on a newspaper publisher and declaring that you want to be a drama critic because, etc., is not likely to get you a job. You're supposed to know what makes a newspaper tick before you can enjoy the proud and happy estate of being a critic.

OF WHAT VALUE IS A SCHOOL OF JOURNALISM COURSE?

Answer: Unless you happen to have attended a school that commands such prestige that its honor graduates are sent for by certain newspapers, having attended a school of journalism is of little practical value.

So You Want to Be a Drama Critic?

Similarly, the fact that you have "taken" a great many courses on drama criticism at a school of journalism conveys little if any significance to a hard-boiled newspaperman.

As far as helping you get a job as a drama critic on a newspaper is concerned, the fact that you have studied drama criticism at a school of journalism will not mean a thing.

WHAT INFLUENCE DOES A DRAMA CRITIC HAVE?

Answer: The New York drama critics are a powerful force in the Broadway theatre.

The early weeks of the engagement of a Broadway production can make or break the show. Unless a producer has a great deal of money to spend in building up a show, he must depend on his attraction winning the attention of a paying audience immediately in order to survive.

When the critics "razz" a play, the chances for the play running become extremely weak. Each of the critics on the New York dailies commands a reading public that follows his opinion on a play. When the reader's favorite critic condemns a play, the chances are that the reader will not spend money to see the show. In addition, the Broadway ticket-brokers, having no real opinions of their own, read the notices to discover whether a play is any good. The ticket-brokers are extremely important to the Broadway producers, since they sell tickets. The ticket-brokers are not likely to recommend a play to their customers if the drama critics do not like the play.

There are occasions when a producer will keep a play running despite the fact that the critics may not have liked it. Since the opinions of the drama critics, when all is said and done, are only what a few men think personally about a play, there is always the chance that they may be wrong and that the play can please an audience. There have been a number of cases on Broadway where plays opened to a poor critical reception and went on lamely for a few weeks, gradually climbing in public favor until they proceeded to make fortunes. "East Is West", "Abie's Irish Rose", and, more recently, "Tobacco Road", are all examples of this phenomenon in the Broadway theatre. They are usually referred to as "freak" successes, although the producers of such "hits" prefer to think that it was their judgment and perseverance over all obstacles that brought success.

However, the spectacle of a play making money over the veto of the drama critics is no longer familiar in the Broadway theatre. The general taste of the theatregoing public is at a considerably higher level than it was some years back. Perhaps the advent of talking pictures, which offer a glittering entertainment at low prices, has had something to do with this, perhaps it's just that audiences have grown more sophisticated

So You Want to Be a Drama Critic?

with the times. But the old days when a critic could honestly dislike a bad play and say so in print, only to observe the play become successful with the public, are over, except in isolated cases.

A set of "rave" notices from the drama critics spells at least some measure of success for a new play and usually brings the producer of a play immediate capacity business. Weak notices from the drama critics almost invariably means death to a play, or, at best, a lame engagement and financial losses. An outright "panning" will cause a show to close almost immediately.

The drama critics in New York sit in judgment on a play. Their decisions are usually final.

WHY ARE CRITICS SOMETIMES ATTACKED BY PRODUCERS?

Answer: For the simple reason that a producer is in the *business* of selling an entertainment to a paying audience. He puts his own money into a show, or else he goes to great trouble to raise the money.

A producer who puts money into a show usually believes in what he is doing. He goes through untold agonies while casting the play and during the rehearsal and try-out periods of production. He may devote weeks and months to preparing a production. He may have thousands of dollars at stake in the investment. He may believe fervently that he has a great "property."

Along come the drama critics and they may hoot his show out of court, not always in the most gentle verbiage.

Producers do not always agree with the opinions of the critics. When they find themselves out of pocket financially and physically exhausted from the labors of the production, they may easily become furious and object to the fact that a limited body of people should guide the pocketbooks of the paying public.

It so happens that a drama critic is not concerned with how much money a producer has invested in a play or how hard he worked to produce the play. The drama critic can only review what he sees and write what he thinks.

It is sometimes difficult for a producer to reconcile himself to that point of view. That's why occasionally some irate producer will write a letter to the Sunday section of the *New York Times*, expressing in no uncertain terms what he thinks of the critics.

DO THE NEW YORK CRITICS KNOW THE PEOPLE THEY WRITE ABOUT?

Answer: It's practically impossible to work at a job and not know at least some of your fellow-workers.

The New York drama critics, in a sense, are employees of the Broadway theatre. It's difficult for them not to know at least a few people in the theatre.

The problem of a drama critic who is required to review a performance given by someone he knows personally is a ticklish one. But, by and large, the New York drama critics manage to be impersonal in their reviews. It is true that sometimes they play favorites and are more lenient with some workers in the theatre than with others. A producer or a playwright with a distinguished record in the theatre is occasionally spared critical abuse for a weak effort, though he will not be praised for it.

There are some actors in the Broadway theatre who invariably command the affection and praise of the critics, sometimes not altogether deservedly in the opinion of those who work in the theatre; but not until they have come over the rocky road of years and years in the theatre, having known the taste of bitter failure and struggle.

Finally, a play can be damned with faint praise just as effectively as with coals of fire. Sometimes the critics will let a friend down easily this way, knowing that the final result will be the same, a failure.

WHAT ARE THE ADVANTAGES OF REVIEWING AN OPENING PERFORMANCE?

Answer: The entire production of a play is aimed at the opening night. Producers, directors, and particularly, actors, prepare all their efforts for the première performance, since that has become traditional in the theatre.

It is also traditional in the theatre for the critics to attend the opening performance so that their reviews about the play can appear in the papers the next day, reporting what has come to town.

As a result, actors usually give their best performance on the opening night, or at least they try to give their best. As a result, the play is usually performed to its keenest advantage since the cast is aware of the importance of the occasion.

On the other hand, the strain of the opening night sometimes has the reverse effect on some actors. A single unfortunate slip, bringing a ripple of laughter at an unexpected place in the action, may be ruinous to an actor's entire performance.

Perhaps the most vicious factor in an opening night performance is the audience. The Broadway first-night crowd is a cruel, cold body and they come into the theatre with a jaded "show-me" attitude, unless they are coming to see the work of a favorite. On such occasions they can be the reverse of hypercritical and lean over backward in blind enthusiasm.

The Broadway "first-nighters" are a treacherous body of theatregoers. The critics are frequently hard pressed to remain impersonal in the midst of a strongly prejudiced audience.

Try to warm up to a play when the audience is frigid.

Or try to remain detached when everybody around you in a theatre is cheering!

WHAT ARE THE ADVANTAGES OF REVIEWING A SECOND NIGHT PERFORMANCE?

Answer: There are some critics who prefer to attend the second night performance of a play to avoid the opening night hysteria, considering the second performance a fairer test for the actors.

However, when a cast has pitched its efforts for the opening night, there is often a tendency to let down on the second night and a performance that only the night before has been full of tension and spirit may become sluggish.

But when a play is downright bad, the chances are it's just as bad the second night as it was the first. The critic's first concern theoretically is the quality of the play, not its performance. A good play should stand up under any kind of a performance.

DO CRITICS PAY FOR THEIR TICKETS?

Answer: It was Robert Garland who once referred to the drama critics as "those who go down the aisles on passes".

The critics do not pay for their tickets. In fact, the press agents send them the best seats in the house for nothing. When a critic wants to see a play a second or even a third time, the press agent is delighted to send him as many tickets as he wants.

There have been notable cases when certain drama critics have been barred from the theatre by producers who have objected to the damaging effects of their reviews. In such cases, the critic who has been "barred" is not able even to purchase tickets for the attraction, a situation that does not occur often. Most producers depend on the reviews of the drama critics and always keep their free list open to the press.

ARE CRITICS PLAYWRIGHTS?

Answer: A fine critic of painting does not have to be a great painter himself to understand and praise great painting or to attack bad painting.

The same analogy holds true in the theatre.

"Can you do better yourself?" is not an adequate reply to a critic who does not like a play or a performance. The ability to write a play or to act does not necessarily go hand in hand with the ability to criticize.

In fact, several of the New York drama critics have tried their hand at playwriting with mediocre results. When a critic writes a play, and has it produced, it's a Roman holiday for the producers, for he's getting a taste of his own medicine.

By the same token, a playwright, as a rule, is not necessarily a well informed or intelligent critic!

SECTION IX

WHAT OPPORTUNITIES ARE THERE OUTSIDE OF NEW YORK?

"Professional baseball has its minor leagues in which promising talent is developed. The theatre once had approximately the same service performed by companies touring with past successes, and by the resident stock companies. Stock companies have always been considered the theatre's training school, as metropolitan newspapermen regard country and small town newspapers as training schools for their profession.

"But in the past few years there has been little opportunity for work in these fields for anybody, as touring companies and stock companies have decreased to an alarming extent.

"The situation which has resulted is serious for the theatre as well as for actors and those who aspire to become actors. For if, in the next few years, there is not a decided revival of the road and of stock we shall have to devise some other method of preparing the candidates for our profession."

— FRANK GILLMORE, *President of Actors' Equity Association, in a letter to the author*

WHAT OPPORTUNITIES ARE THERE OUTSIDE OF NEW YORK?

Answer: After you have surveyed the hazards and complexities of the Broadway scene, you may very reasonably wonder where else you may seek an honorable opportunity to express your talents in the theatre.

How are you going to find out if you have any talent, before you put all your chips on attempting a career in the professional theatre? Where can you learn your job of work? Who will teach you?

The broad fields for one who wants to try his hand in the theatre, but who is unwilling or unable to seek an opportunity directly on Broadway, are threefold. There are the summer theatres, the little theatres, and the groups that function at universities and colleges.

However, remember that the theatre off Broadway invariably assumes some tinge of the amateur. While the work of the amateur in the theatre may sometimes be even superior to that of the professional, categorically there is an enormous difference. Even in the summer theatres, which have a direct connection with Broadway in personnel, the working conditions are far from being fully professional. You can be a "wow" in the "sticks" when audiences are friendly and tolerant, and a complete "bust" on Broadway.

The truth of the matter is that experience in the fields that exist off Broadway is no real test of your ability for Broadway.

WHAT IS A LITTLE THEATRE?

Answer: There are thousands upon thousands of groups across the country who devote themselves to amateur theatricals. Practically every little church has a class or group that devotes itself to "putting on a play". Women's clubs, fraternal lodges, political clubs, all kinds of societies, have their members who will get together once or twice a year and give some sort of an entertainment.

Eliminate these from our examination, for they are not the so-called little theatres.

The little theatre, or community theatre movement, is an offshoot of the old amateur theatrical societies which have flourished in this country for several generations, groups of amateurs organized and devoted solely to the staging and presentation of plays. Originally these theatrical societies merely aped Broadway by presenting amateur versions of Broadway successes.

With the road bristling with activity and every city in the nation visited regularly by touring companies of Broadway actors, the local community amateur societies did not feel called upon to do any creative work. There was sufficient professional activity to satisfy the demands of the provinces.

The decline of the road stirred these community

What Opportunities Outside of New York?

groups to a definite kind of theatre activity of their own. As far back as 1911, however, the Plays and Players Society in Philadelphia decided to break with the accepted amateur tradition of imitating Broadway and ventured into the experiment of staging several literate plays ignored by Broadway and the professional theatre of that day.

This was one of the indications of a birth of the little theatre movement.

Today we have the spectacle of hundreds of amateur groups, located in every important city of the nation, engaged in the production of "interesting" plays. The little theatre does not always scorn Broadway. In fact, its stock in trade consists largely of revivals of Broadway successes, often in extremely effective productions. The point about the little theatre is that, at its best, there is a certain *esprit de corps* and integrity in its organization that is distinctly professional.

Whereas, on Broadway, discipline is based on two counts, the tradition that the "show must go on" and the fact that the workers of the professional theatre are paid employees who can be discharged by their employers, in the typical little theatre there is a group enthusiasm and singleness of purpose that often makes for good, clean-cut theatre.

In short, while the little theatre movement is composed of amateurs, they are amateurs in the finest sense. They are engaged in their work for the sheer fun and satisfaction of doing it. Their results vary according to their talents, of course, but often the results are splendid.

Some of the greatest athletes in the world are amateurs who never enter into the professional ranks because they happen to have other interests in life beside sports. The same is true of the little theatres. Many a splendid actor and director is content to stay with some little theatre group, without devoting any thought to entering the professional theatre. And, by the same token, there are many hopelessly bad actors and perhaps limited directors who are equally content to enjoy themselves in a little theatre without ever being troubled by thoughts of having to make a living out of it.

A little theatre is an organization of theatre workers who are non-professional, in the sense that they are not paid for their work, interested in rehearsing and staging productions which they do entirely themselves. Most little theatres command community following and interest. They vary in resources and equipment, from organizations that have large theatres with rehearsal halls, elaborate equipment for the building and painting of scenery, modern stages and paraphernalia, etc., to humble little groups who work in restricted quarters and are able to give performances only to tiny audiences.

Approximately ninety-five per cent. of all the peo-

What Opportunities Outside of New York?

ple engaged in the little theatre movement are not concerned with entering the professional Broadway theatre.

WHAT IS A SUMMER THEATRE?

Answer: Beginning with about June first of each year, a great portion of the Broadway population moves out into the country to give performances of plays in remodelled barns, assembly halls, community centers, churches, and playshops located in dozens of little hamlets from the celebrated rockbound coast of Maine as far south as Virginia and extending west into Pennsylvania.

The summer theatre is predicated on a pleasant outdoor existence for a professional company that can hope to play to an audience of summer residents in the various communities in which, or near which, the theatre is located.

Most summer theatres are organized and operated on the proverbial "shoe-string". Salaries are tiny, expenses are low, productions are skimpy and makeshift, with their managers dependent on enlisting the interest of a paying audience to cover expenses and keep the company alive.

As a result, many a summer company starts out bravely and "folds up" after one or two weeks, because no well-paying audience will bother to turn up at the doors.

There are other summer theatres, more elaborately

equipped and better financed, which in some cases enjoy the interest and support of a summer community.

The average length of a season for a summer theatre is about ten weeks and productions are usually performed on a stock basis; that is, a new production is presented each week.

The entire summer theatre business is a comparatively recent development in the professional theatre and is partially the result of the fact that many workers in the theatre have been unable to find an opportunity on Broadway and have gone out into the country each summer in search of a chance to work and win a reputation.

Thus far, the summer theatre, unlike the little theatre movement, has not paid its way. Most summer theatres lose money for their management, a few break even, and extremely few make a profit.

Yet the summer theatre is founded primarily on a professional point of view. Its workers must be paid at least something in order to live and it is almost entirely aimed at Broadway. Many actors who go to summer theatres for a pittance hope to be seen by visiting Broadway producers. The same is true for many summer theatre directors who hope to attract attention through their activity in this field. Many young producers try to test previously unproduced plays in the summer theatres in the hope of unearth-

What Opportunities Outside of New York?

ing one worth doing on Broadway, either through their own efforts or through enlisting the interest of someone able to finance them. Some summer theatre managers try out plays for Broadway producers in the hope of acquiring a small "piece of the show" if subsequently presented on Broadway.

Essentially the summer theatres are highly imitative of Broadway and since the working conditions and general environment are largely amateur, the entire summer theatre movement is basically insecure.

However, it is the only field in the theatre off Broadway that is allied to Broadway and it may grow in stature and results with the years. It is certainly safe to state that the summer theatre is here to stay. Each year a new crop of them springs up and annually some of the older companies reveal better productions.

WHAT ARE THE LEADING LITTLE THEATRES?

Answer: No one person as yet has been able to review the efforts of every little theatre group in the country, although such men as Kenneth Macgowan and Barrett H. Clark have made brave and exhaustive attempts to survey the efforts of many companies and have noted some of the results they have observed.

There must be easily a thousand little theatres or community playhouses in the United States, probably considerably more. Any attempt to compare the activities of these groups is clearly a formidable task and it becomes difficult to score a limited few as the distinct leaders in the field.

However, there are a number of extremely well equipped organizations who have done more than creditable work and who have presented a number of extremely ambitious productions that might be compared favorably with productions in the professional Broadway theatre.

The Cleveland Playhouse, the Pasadena Community Playhouse, the Dallas Little Theatre, the Seattle Repertory Playhouse, the Omaha Playhouse and Le Petit Théâtre du Vieux Carré in New Orleans are a few of the so-called little theatre companies which have attracted national attention.

An attempt to single out these groups as notably outstanding, however, is unfair to the little theatre movement as a whole, since it is founded on the fact that any group of competent people, so minded, can form and operate a little theatre group that can eventually present reasonably satisfying productions which may gradually acquire a high degree of excellence.

If you want to enter a little theatre, the chances are there is one in your home town or in a city not far from you.

Incidentally, there is nothing to stop you from starting a little theatre of your own, and always the chance that you may start one that will eventually became first-rate.

What Opportunities Outside of New York?

WHAT ARE THE LEADING SUMMER THEATRES?

Answer: Any attempt to answer this question in absolute terms would also be misleading. There are really no "leading" summer theatres. There are only some which are a little better financed and equipped than others, and which may happen to enjoy better than average community support.

Of the summer theatres which have been in existence in the last few years, there are some which have been consistently able to attract well known Broadway actors as members of the company and which have presented extremely competent productions under the prevailing conditions.

By and large, the "leading" summer theatres are those which are located in resorts where they attract the interest and support of fashionable audiences composed, in the main, of the vacationing "carriage trade".

Among the summer theatres which have been performing for several years, more or less successfully, are The Country Playhouse at Westport and the New York Players at Ivorytown, in Connecticut; the Mount Desert Playhouse at Bar Harbor, the Ogunquit Playhouse at Ogunquit, and the Lakewood Theatre at Skowhegan, in Maine; the Cape Playhouse at Dennis, the Berkshire Playhouse at Stockbridge, and the Beach Theatre at West Falmouth, in Massachusetts; the Red

228 *So You Want to Go Into the Theatre?*

Barn Theatre at Locust Valley, the Westchester Playhouse at Mount Kisco, the Hampton Players at Southhampton, the Country Theatre at Suffern, and the Maverick Theatre at Woodstock, in New York; and the Newport Casino in Rhode Island.

The full list of summer theatres that operate each summer is staggering. Many of them are located within a few miles of each other. Some engage resident companies, some engage actors for a single play or for several plays. Some summer theatres engage guest stars for one play, some follow the old stock company system of having leading men and women in the resident company. Some engage free lance directors, most of them are directed by the people who manage the companies.

There are no absolute rules or generalizations that may be applied to the summer theatres as a class. They are sporadic organizations and all of them present exceptions to any rule that may be devised.

The Stage Magazine devotes several issues each year to listing all the summer theatres which announce plans. Also the New York daily papers, beginning with about May of each year, all carry the announcements of activity issued by the dozens of summer theatre aspirants.

A permanent record of the summer theatres defies statement, for the summer theatres come and go like the wind and there is never any telling when even

What Opportunities Outside of New York? 229
what appear to be the established companies may vanish from the scene.

HOW DO YOU GET A JOB IN A SUMMER THEATRE?

Answer: This is another cockeyed, confusing business.

To begin with, you must first locate the director or manager of a summer theatre, before you can ask for a job in his company.

Only a handful of the summer theatre managers maintain New York offices or even residences.

There are a few helpful hints, however, which may be cited.

Most of the summer theatre companies are organized in New York beginning about May of each year. (Of course, some of the summer theatre managers have their companies picked from people they know long before that.) As a result, these various managers come to New York and locate in some producer's office, or in a hotel, or in a casting agent's office.

Watch the New York papers and, as soon as an announcement of a summer theatre's plans appears, first approach Actors' Equity and inquire whether the location of the manager is known.

Next visit all the casting agents.

Scour the various meeting places along Broadway. (These have already been cited.) You may pick up information from actors who have heard where various summer theatre companies are being cast.

Finally, write letters, asking for an interview, to the managers of the summer theatres that have announced activity. Address your communications to the town where the theatre is located. In most cases, forwarding addresses have been left with local post-offices and such mail may reach the person you have addressed. A list of some of the summer theatres and their managing directors is given in the back of this book.

If you never receive an answer to your letter, don't be surprised. It's possible that the theatre is no longer in existence, or, even though production plans have been announced, they may have been abandoned. Again, the jobs may all be filled.

When you boil it down, landing a job in a summer theatre is like nothing so much as searching for a needle in a haystack. It's pretty hard to get a job when you can't even locate the person who gives the employment!

WHAT KIND OF JOBS ARE THERE IN A SUMMER THEATRE?

Answer: The summer theatres in a sense resemble the little theatres, since everybody pitches in to do whatever work is necessary around the company. No task is too humble to assume in a summer theatre. And don't be deceived by the notion that you will enjoy a vacation in the country when you go off with a summer theatre. You may have a good time, but the chances are that you'll work your head off. Putting on

What Opportunities Outside of New York?
a show in a week with limited equipment is a real job.

In a summer theatre you can expect to act, direct, design scenery, build and paint scenery, sew costumes, locate properties and furniture for love or money, sell tickets, distribute posters, do publicity, sweep the theatre, sell punch and refreshments, entertain local inhabitants and persuade them to attend performances, type parts, lick stamps, make costumes, or cook.

Any or all of these duties may be assigned to you in a summer theatre and all of these items must be done by someone in all summer theatres.

That is the major difference between the summer theatres and Broadway. Only in a few summer theatres are there any union regulations such as are to be found on Broadway. As a result, you may be called upon to do all sorts of odd jobs necessary in the operation of a theatre.

IS A LITTLE THEATRE BETTER THAN BROADWAY?

Answer: It all depends on what you're looking for.

From the complete theatric point of view, the best production in a little theatre will never match the quality of the best production on Broadway. The Broadway theatre, despite all its faults and foibles, is frequently the finest theatre in the world. The little theatre movement can never hope to match the efforts of Jed Harris or the Theatre Guild or Katharine Cornell at their top best. The Broadway theatre can be deeply beautiful esthetically and peerless technically.

But, on the other hand, if it's a chance for self-expression in the theatre that you're seeking, or the opportunity to experiment freely, the little theatre movement has a great many things to offer. Your errors will not be costly or beyond repair. You will not be faced by stern professional critics or cold first-night audiences with a chip on their collective shoulders. You won't be in the theatre to make a living, with the sharp terror of failure staring you in the face.

HOW MUCH MONEY CAN YOU EARN IN A LITTLE THEATRE?

Answer: The little theatre movement is not predicated on its workers making a living. When you work in a little theatre, usually you do it in your spare time and have some other source of revenue, so that it becomes something of a hobby. The Cleveland Playhouse, and perhaps one or two others, does pay some members of the company small salaries, but this is entirely the exception to the rule.

However, in every little theatre, particularly those with ambitious production plans, there must be some one person who, more or less, devotes his entire time to the group. This person is usually the director. There are some directors of little theatres who earn salaries for their work. Usually they are the original organizers of their groups, although in some cases interested

What Opportunities Outside of New York? members of a community have organized their little theatre and offered the position of director to an outsider.

You can organize your own little theatre and, through a common understanding with the other members of your group, earn a salary for your efforts. Practically the only paying job open in connection with the little theatre is that of director, who is engaged usually by the season and receives anywhere from $1,200 to about $5,000 a year. The average salary among the better type of little theatres is about $2,000 per season. It is, however, extremely hard to get such a job and very few recognized professional directors are used in this capacity. In a few of the larger little theatres an assistant director is paid, but usually this is someone who has worked up from the ranks.

If one is looking for experience either as actor, designer, stage-manager, or director, it is somewhat easier to become attached to one of these groups if you don't require a salary. More rarely, jobs can be obtained in connection with the college and university theatres, many of which are as well equipped and as efficient as the little theatres.

In general, there is no money to be made working in a little theatre.

IS THERE A CHANCE TO DIRECT IN A LITTLE THEATRE?
Answer: The chances are limited.

Most little theatres are managed by people who are in the movement because they themselves want to direct.

However, if you are accepted by a little theatre group and have talent as a director, you may eventually enjoy the opportunity of directing a production.

The most likely way to become a director of a little theatre is to form a group of your own.

TO DESIGN? TO BUILD SCENERY? TO PAINT SCENERY?

Answer: Every little theatre needs people who will assume the burden of preparing a physical production. Building and painting scenery, making costumes, assembling properties and everything needed for the production of a play, is work that must be done by members of the group.

In most little theatres there are committees assigned to this technical work and ample opportunity for anyone interested to try his hand at it.

If you have unusual ideas as a scene designer, the little theatre offers you rich opportunities for experiment.

OF WHAT VALUE IS SUCH EXPERIENCE IN NEW YORK?

Answer: Precious little.

You may become expert at building and painting scenery in a little theatre, but Broadway will have

What Opportunities Outside of New York?

none of you unless you can become a member of the Scenic Artists or stage-hands' unions.

As for your experience as an actor, director, scene designer, or business manager, it will make very little impression on Broadway producers, no matter how famous the little theatre with which you have worked. Broadway considers anyone from a little theatre an "amateur". On Broadway, that's no compliment.

CAN YOU MAKE A REPUTATION IN A LITTLE THEATRE?

Answer: After a limited fashion.

You can command respect in your own community and enjoy a certain prestige with the leaders of other little theatres, particularly if you happen to be a director with a successful record. Certain little theatre directors have achieved a national reputation and, because of their long association with their own groups outside New York, are known and respected, including Gilmor Brown, Jasper Deeter, Frederic McConnell, and Oliver Hinsdell, to mention a few.

But, at best, it doesn't mean much on Broadway.

CAN YOU MAKE A REPUTATION IN A SUMMER THEATRE?

Answer: Yes.

Broadway is in more or less direct connection with the summer theatres. Broadway producers visit a great many of the summer show-shops to see productions.

As a result, actors and directors are frequently "discovered" in this fashion, leading to Broadway engagements.

Also an actor may be able to persuade casting agents to come to the country and view a particular performance and interest the agents toward securing Broadway engagements.

Again, there is always the possibility that the manager or director of a summer theatre may become active on Broadway and the members of his summer company benefit directly.

A good stage manager or scene designer may prove himself in a summer theatre and subsequently obtain work on Broadway.

HOW MUCH BACKING DO YOU NEED TO START A LITTLE OR SUMMER THEATRE?

Answer: You can start a little theatre with no money at all of your own, by organizing a group where everyone chips in a little money, or by persuading leading people in your community to pledge some money or to buy subscriptions for a series of plays.

A little theatre can be as "little" as you want to make it at first and from that point it can grow as the work of your group matures. You can start in a community center, a school auditorium, a lodge, or wherever you can find some sort of a stage to play on, with room for an audience to sit. Eventually, you may be able to build a theatre of your own.

If you want to organize a summer theatre, however, your problem is much more complex. You should have at least a few thousand dollars in "backing" to begin such a venture, for, no matter how economical your budget may be, there will be certain fixed expenses that you cannot avoid. The operating of a summer theatre is a professional venture and as soon as you enter the professional theatre, you must have financing and be prepared to lose it and still carry on, or else "fold up."

The moment you are faced with the problem of paying salaries to a cast and staff, you must also count on selling your tickets consistently to stay alive. That means advertising and publicity, which costs money, plus all the expenses that are incurred in the production and operating of any professional play, even though they are on a reduced scale.

In addition, the field of summer theatres is so overcrowded that the chances of making one pay its own way are woefully slim. The competition is stiff.

You can start a little theatre on practically nothing but your enthusiasm and talent, if you are energetic and can arouse the enthusiasm and talent of others in your community. But if you start a summer theatre, you're in "show business"!

WHAT OPENINGS ARE THERE WITH COLLEGES AND UNIVERSITIES?

Answer: According to Barrett H. Clark, there are approximately 700 colleges and universities with approximately 40,000 students, that offer courses in dramatic work and present regular dramatic productions.

Of this number approximately 100 have well equipped theatres and competent producing staffs, and perhaps a total of 200 that present ambitious productions.

The drama activities in the American colleges and universities are indisputably a wide and impressive field for anyone who wants to do theatre work. Institutions such as Yale, Pennsylvania State College, New York University, the University of Pennsylvania, Harvard, Princeton, Northwestern, the University of Iowa, the University of Washington, Vassar, Syracuse, the University of Chicago, Wisconsin, Ohio State, Columbia, Dartmouth, Western Reserve, and Grinnell, to quote a few, all present a distinct opportunity for anyone who wants to try his hand in the theatre.

Many of these schools have blazed the way for experimental production. Playwrights such as Lynn Riggs, Paul Green, Martin Flavin and Maxwell Anderson have seen world premières of their plays given by drama groups at universities and colleges.

The possibility of becoming an instructor in a university or college drama department, upon being graduated from an institution of learning, always exists. There are also cases of men who have come out of such departments and performed service on Broadway, including Milton Smith of Columbia University and Alexander Dean of Yale University. There are many others who have come out of college groups and become established on Broadway as actors, directors, scene designers, stage managers and producers.

If you are interested in the theatre, your work at college can be valuable experience.

To cite a few impressive names, Franchot Tone, Bretaigne Windust, Katharine Hepburn, Osgood Perkins, and John Beal are among those who started their theatre work at college.

But, like the little theatre, if you come to Broadway with a background of theatre activity at some college or university, you will still be nothing but a tyro on Broadway and you will have to go through the mill just like anyone else before you can get anywhere.

DO YOU WANT TO GO INTO THE THEATRE?
Answer: First, ask yourself why and then check the facts.

If you find you just "like" the theatre, you will be wise to confine your efforts to some amateur form.

In order to come into the Broadway theatre, and that is the only professional theatre we have in this country, you must have tremendous ego and self-confidence. You must be prepared for all sorts of humiliation. You must have enormous courage and a magnificent sense of humor. You must have genuine talent and be able to prove it not only to others, but to yourself, as well.

You will be bucking a business where the mathematical odds are loaded heavily against you and it may take you a long time before you know you are licked. You will be faced by "type" casting, the need of reputation, small average earnings, the fact that most plays on Broadway are failures, that there is little opportunity for newcomers, keen competition, practically no chance to learn your job thoroughly, and the fact that very few people will care one hoot about whether you succeed or not.

If you want to come into the theatre, you're gambling and, when you gamble, you may lose.

END

APPENDIX

BROADWAY GLOSSARY

"Angel" .... anyone who puts up money for a show.
"Apron" .... the section of the stage in front of the act-curtain.
"Belly laugh" .... solid laughter from an audience.
"The bird" .... an eloquent vocal sign of displeasure from a member of the audience.
"Bit" .... a small speaking part in a play.
"Blow up" .... to become disconcerted on stage and forget one's lines.
"The book" .... the prompt-manuscript.
"The boys" .... the ticket-brokers.
"Break up" .... actors sometimes deliberately break each other up in their lines by playing practical jokes on each other during a performance.
"Business" .... any physical activity an actor has to do on the stage.
"Carriage trade" ..... fashionable theatregoers who arrive in limousines.
"Clean house" .... sold-out audience.
"Coffee and cakes" .... a small salary.

"Count the house".... the duty which confronts the company manager in the box-office each performance. Also what an actor will sometimes do during a performance, to the disgust of a director.
"Cyc" .... a cyclorama or back-drop.
"Dark house"......... a theatre which is closed and without an attraction.
"Dead wood"......... the tickets which are left unsold after a performance.
"Doubling" .... playing more than one part.
"Doubling in brass"... doing more than one job for a single salary.
"Dry up"............. when an actor forgets his lines completely and causes a stage-wait.
"Fly it".............. the order given when scenery is lifted on ropes into the flies.
"Folded up".......... a show that has closed.
"Four walls"......... renting a theatre on a lease.
"The ghost walks"..... pay-day.
"Grip" .... an ordinary stage-hand who is assistant to the chief carpenter.
"Half hour".......... the warning given by the stage manager a half hour before curtain time.
"Ham" .... either a vain or a bad actor.
"Hanging the show" ... setting up the scenery.
"Hard wood"......... exchange-tickets used in the box-office when cutting the price of a ticket.

Appendix

"Hook up" . . . . the way a show is budgeted, particularly the relation of the production cost to the operating cost.

"How many sides?" . . . . the number of pages in an actor's part.

"Ice" . . . . the premium collected on tickets sold above the listed box-office price.

"In the red" . . . . a show that is losing money.

"Joe's" . . . . the Leblang cut-rate ticket agency.

"Laid an egg" . . . . a show that has been a failure.

"Lay 'em in the aisles" . . making an audience roar with laughter.

"The list" . . . . the pass-list.

"Milk jump" . . . . a town that can be reached on tour only by an arduous train-trip, usually in the early morning.

"Milking it dry" . . . . getting as many laughs as possible out of a scene or a line.

"Mugging" . . . . over-doing facial pantomime.

"Notices" . . . . the reviews.

"Nut" . . . . the production cost of a show.

"Off the nut" . . . . when the show is making a clear profit.

"On the dog" . . . . an out-of-town try-out.

"One night stand" . . . . . an out-of-town engagement of one performance.

"Opening cold" . . . . opening on Broadway without a try-out.

"Paper" . . . . passes.

"Paper the house"..... making a show look like a success by giving away passes.
"Piece of the show" .... ownership in a production.
"Places, please!"....... the order given by the stage manager to the cast just before the curtain rises.
"Props" .... any tangible objects which the cast must handle during a performance.
"Raves" .... ecstatic reviews.
"The razz"........... unanimously bad reviews.
"Shoe-string" .... a play that has been produced with very little money.
"Sitting on their hands" .... an unresponsive audience.
"Smash" .... a show that plays to standing room.
"Sock" .... ditto.
"Split week".......... an out-of-town engagement lasting a half week.
"Sticks" .... the road.
"Take a call"......... the order to take a bow.
"Throw it away"...... the director's suggestion that an actor place no emphasis on a line to make it effective.
"Throw me the line" ... a request for prompting.
"Top it"............. the method by which an actor builds a scene through picking up a cue and increasing the volume and intensity of his own speech.
"Trouper" .... an experienced actor.
"Trouping" .... going on tour.

Appendix

"Turkey" ....a rank failure.
"Twenty four sheet"...a large billboard used for advertising.
"Two for one"........a printed pass that permits one to buy two tickets for the price of one. These passes are often distributed publicly when a play is a failure.
"Upstaging" ....forcing an actor to turn his back on the audience by moving upstage from him.
"Walk on"............an extra who has no lines to read.
"Wing it"............going on to play a part without knowing the lines and being prompted from the wings.

NEW YORK PRODUCERS

(Note: Producers frequently move their offices. However, they usually leave forwarding addresses.)

George Abbott	220 West 42nd St.
Charles Abramson	1 East 54th St.
Hyman Adler	156 West 44th St.
Helen Arthur	22 East 55th St.
Frederick Ayer	1560 Broadway
Theron Bamberger	132 West 43rd St.
Albert Bannister	220 West 48th St.
Baruch & Pearson	Paramount Bldg.
Martin Beck	302 West 45th St.
Leonard Bergman	214 West 42nd St.
J. P. Bickerton, Jr.	220 West 42nd St.
Bela Blau	234 West 44th St.

Gustav Blum	11 West 42nd St.
Wm. A. Brady	137 West 48th St.
Bulgakov & Spiller	℅ Wm. Morris Agency, 701 7th Ave.
Courtney Burr	226 West 42nd St.
Bushar & Tuerk	137 West 48th St.
Earl Carroll	7 West 44th St.
Delos Chappell	Hecksher Bldg.
George M. Cohan	152 West 42nd St.
Irving Cooper	1430 Broadway
Katharine Cornell	1270 6th Ave.
Harry Cort	202 West 58th St.
Curtis & Hoagland	1619 Broadway
Alfred de Liagre, Jr.	11 West 42nd St.
Eddie Dowling	St. James Theatre
Denis Dufor	1564 Broadway
Philip Dunning	220 West 42nd St.
Erlanger Productions	214 West 42nd St.
Chester Erskin	356 East 57th St.
Henry Forbes	1430 Broadway
George Ford	55 West 44th St.
Vinton Freedley	250 West 52nd St.
William B. Friedlander	220 West 48th St.
Charles Frohman, Inc.	℅ James Reilly, Paramount Bldg.
Daniel Frohman	152 West 46th St.
Crosby Gaige	229 West 42nd St.
Herman Gantvoort	234 West 44th St.
Morris Gest	71 East 52nd St.
John Golden	Lincoln Hotel
Max Gordon	214 West 42nd St.
Morris Green	1482 Broadway
Sam Grisman	Paramount Bldg.

Appendix

Group Theatre	246 West 44th St.
Theodore Hammerstein	1564 Broadway
Walter Hampden	Ridgefield, Conn.
Forrest C. Haring	137 West 48th St.
Sidney Harmon	1430 Broadway
Jed Harris	1430 Broadway
Sam H. Harris	239 West 45th St.
Wm. Harris, Jr.	139 West 44th St.
Walter Hart	1430 Broadway
Walter Hartwig	152 West 46th St.
Richard Herndon	226 West 47th St.
Mack Hilliard	229 West 42nd St.
Arthur Hopkins	236 West 45th St.
A. L. Jones	1482 Broadway
Messmore Kendall	1639 Broadway
Thomas Kilpatrick	234 West 44th St.
George Kondolf	214 West 42nd St.
Krimsky & Cochrane	229 West 42nd St.
Lawrence Langner	245 West 52nd St.
Mrs. Tillie Leblang	1482 Broadway
Eve LeGallienne	103 West 14th St.
Jules J. Leventhal	125 West 45th St.
Frank Mandel	67 West 44th St.
Mayer & Green	9 East 46th St.
Guthrie McClintic	1270 6th Ave.
Elizabeth Miehle	234 West 44th St.
Gilbert Miller	124 West 43rd St.
Raymond Moore	Lincoln Hotel
Harry Moses	1430 Broadway
Brock Pemberton	244 West 44th St.
Potter & Haight	234 West 44th St.
Laurence Rivers Inc.	19 West 44th St.
Billy Rose	120 West 42nd St.

Laurence Schwab	234 West 44th St.
Lee & J. J. Shubert	225 West 44th St.
Milton Shubert	225 West 44th St.
Herman Shumlin	229 West 42nd St.
Leonard Sillman	229 West 42nd St.
Rowland Stebbins	19 West 44th St.
Paul Streger	654 Madison Ave.
Theatre of Action	42 East 12th St.
Theatre Guild Inc.	245 West 52nd St.
Theatre Union	103 West 14th St.
Shepard Traube	485 Madison Ave.
George C. Tyler	214 West 42nd St.
James Ullman	1430 Broadway
J. J. Vincent	11 West 42nd St.
Lodewick Vroom	Adelphi Theatre
Charles L. Wagner	511 5th Ave.
Tom Weatherly	137 West 48th St.
Lawrence L. Weber	220 West 48th St.
O. E. Wee	125 West 45th St.
Meyer Weisgall	229 West 42nd St.
Dwight Deere Wiman	137 West 48th St.
A. H. Woods	1270 6th Ave.
Alex Yokel	1585 Broadway

NEW YORK PLAYBROKERS

American Play Co.	33 West 42nd St.
Hans Bartsch	1639 Broadway
Brandt & Brandt	101 Park Ave.
Louis Britwitz	45 West 45th St.
Curtis Brown Ltd.	18 East 48th St.
Co-National Play Co.	1545 Broadway
Bartley Cushing	303 West 42nd St.

Appendix 251

Frieda Fishbein	1482 Broadway
Samuel French Inc.	25 West 45th St.
Myra Furst	16 West 46th St.
General Play Co.	551 5th Ave.
R. L. Giffen	152 West 42nd St.
Edith Gordon	100 West 42nd St.
Leland Hayward	654 Madison Ave.
International Literary Bureau	18 East 48th St.
Alice Kauser	152 West 42nd St.
Carrie Koch	1520 Broadway
Maxim Lieber	545 5th Ave.
Richard J. Madden	33 West 42nd St.
Elizabeth Marbury Inc.	234 West 44th St.
Beatrice Miller	144 East 74th St.
Jessica Miller	1560 Broadway
Ann Miner	65 West 46th St.
Grace Morse	545 5th Ave.
Fleet Munson	743 5th Ave.
Borry Osso	1639 Broadway
Dr. Edmond Pauker	1639 Broadway
Pinker & Morrison	9 East 46th St.
Carl Reed	234 West 44th St.
Maurice S. Richter	15 East 40th St.
Louis Rubsamen	33 West 42nd St.
Leah Salisbury	234 West 44th St.
Henry L. Schiffer	120 West 44th St.
Alexander Sukennikoff	229 West 42nd St.
Ethel C. Taylor	16 West 46th St.
Jessy Trimble	Hotel Shelton
Florence Vincent Inc.	45 West 45th St.
Roy Walling	1482 Broadway
Anne Walters	326 East 71st St.

Ann Watkins	210 Madison Ave.
Cedric Weller	8 West 13th St.
Jean Wick	24 5th Ave.
Laura D. Wilck	1639 Broadway
Audrey Wood	730 5th Ave.
Gertrude Workman	117 East 10th St.
Ida Wyckoff	229 West 42nd St.

NEW YORK CASTING AGENTS

Walter Batchelor	234 West 44th St.
M. S. Bentham	1564 Broadway
Harry Bestry	1493 Broadway
Pauline Boyle	1564 Broadway
Briscoe & Goldsmith	522 5th Ave.
Jane Broder	Times Bldg.
Chamberlain Brown	145 West 45th St.
Pauline Cook	1674 Broadway
Curtis & Allen	RKO Bldg., Rockefeller Center
Edward Davidow	755 7th Ave.
Sara Enright	234 West 44th St.
Leo Fitzgerald	1819 Broadway
Joe Gilbert	145 West 45th St.
Ethel Golden	1587 Broadway
Matt Grau	152 West 42nd St.
Sylvia Hahlo	145 West 58th St.
Max Hart	1560 Broadway
Herbert Hoey	1270 6th Ave.
Richard Huey (colored only)	172 West 135th St.
Lou Irwin	1270 6th Ave.
Al Knight	1560 Broadway

Appendix

Wm. Liebling	RKO Bldg., Rockefeller Center
Lyons & Lyons	Paramount Bldg.
Austina Mason	100 West 42nd St.
Maynard Morris	234 West 44th St.
William Morris Inc.	RKO Bldg., Rockefeller Center
Charles Morrison	Park Central Hotel
Michael Myerberg	113 West 57th St.
Murray Phillips	755 7th Ave.
Richard Pitman	1674 Broadway
Frances Robinson	220 West 42nd St.
Will Roehm	1571 Broadway
Louis Shurr	Paramount Bldg.
Minnie Webster	111 West 57th St.
Dan Winkler	654 Madison Ave.
Wales Winter	152 West 42nd St.
Georgia Wolfe	1482 Broadway
George Wood	1501 Broadway

SUMMER THEATRES

(These theatres have been active in past summers under the managements mentioned, but are subject to change each season. For a complete annual list consult *The Stage Magazine*.)

Connecticut

Greenwich — *Greenwich Playhouse*. Managers, James Ullman and Richard Herndon.

Ivorytown — *The New York Players*. Director, Milton Stiefel.

Madison Beach — *The Post Road Players*. Frederick W. Ayer, Manager.

Niantic — *Crescent Theatre*. Director, Gregory Deane.
Stony Creek — *The Stony Creek Theatre*. Director, Brace Conning.
Westport — *Country Playhouse*. Director, Lawrence Langner.

Delaware

Arden — *The Robin Hood Theatre*. Director, Thelma Chander.

Maine

Bar Harbor — *Bar Harbor Players*. Managing Director, Edwin Whitney Payne.
Kennebunkport — *Garrick Players*. Manager, Dorothy Manners.
Ogunquit — *Ogunquit Playhouse*. Director, Walter Hartwig.
Skowhegan — *Lakewood Theatre*. Director, Melville Burke.

Massachusetts

Cohasset — *South Shore Players*. Director, Alexander Dean.
Dennis — *Cape Playhouse*. Manager, Raymond Moore.
Martha's Vineyard — *Rice Playhouse*. Director, Phidelah Rice.
Provincetown — *Wharf Theatre*. Manager, Margaret Hughes.
Stockbridge — *Berkshire Playhouse*. Director, William Miles.
West Falmouth — *Beach Theatre*. Manager, Luther Greene.
Westford — *Lakeshore Theatre*. Managing Directors, Mr. & Mrs. Franklin Trask.

Appendix 255

New Hampshire

New London — *The Barn Playhouse*. Director, Josephine E. Holmes.

Peterboro — *Peterboro Players*. Manager, Edith Bond Stearns.

Rye Beach — *Farragut Players*. Manager, Donald Towers.

New Jersey

Cape May — *Hilda Spong Players*. Director, Hilda Spong.

Spring Lake — *Monmouth Community Players*. Manager, Hudson Fausset.

New York

Lake Mahopac — *Mahopac Theatre*. Director, Edward Raquello.

Locust Valley — *Red Barn*. Manager, D. A. Doran.

Millbrook — *Millbrook Theatre*. Director, Edward Massey.

Mt. Kisco — *Westchester Playhouse*. Director, Day Tuttle.

Pawling — *Starlight Theatre*. Director, Maryverne Jones.

Scarborough-on-Hudson — *Beechwood Theatre*. Manager, Paul L. Berney.

Suffern — *Country Theatre*. Manager, Robert F. Cutler.

White Plains — *Ridgeway Theatre*. Director, Day Tuttle.

Woodstock — *Maverick Theatre*. Director, Robert Elwyn.

Pennsylvania

Moylan-Rose Valley — *Hedgerow Theatre*. Director, Jasper Deeter.

Nuangola — *Grove Theatre*. Manager, John Ravold.

Rhode Island

Matunick — *Theatre-by-the-Sea*. Director, Halstead Welles.

Newport — *Newport Casino*. Manager, Lillian Barrett.

Vermont

Brattleboro — *Brattleboro Theatre*. Director, Paul Stephenson.

Virginia

Abingdon — *Barber Theatre*. Manager, Robert Porterfield.

SUPPLEMENTARY READINGS

A vast amount of literature has been written about the theatre, but there are some recent works which may be of particular interest in connection with the contents of this book. A selected list includes:

The Billboard "Index", published annually and contains a complete statistical record of each Broadway season.

"Box Office" by JOHN ANDERSON, a shrewd although brief commentary on the show business of today.

"B'way, Inc." by MORTON EUSTIS, full of well-documented facts concerning the commercial theatre.

"Footlights Across America" by KENNETH MACGOWAN, a good account of the non-professional theatre, but is now some ten years out of date.

"Best Plays" by BURNS MANTLE, published annually, containing abbreviated texts of the ten plays selected as "best" by Mr. Mantle and also containing a record of each Broadway season.

"The Drama in English" by WALTER PRICHARD EATON, a compact, intelligent survey of the drama in English-speaking countries.

"How's Your Second Act?" by ARTHUR HOPKINS, an extremely suggestive and somewhat philosophical treatise on the art of directing.

"So You're Writing a Play?" by CLAYTON HAMILTON, safe advice for budding playwrights.

"The Stage Is Set" by LEE SIMONSON, a most provocative book consisting of a series of essays on various aspects of the theatre.

"The Curtain Falls" by JOSEPH VERNER REED, a good-humored account of that producer's experiences in the commercial theatre and why he eventually retired from it.

"A Study of the Modern Drama" by BARRETT H. CLARK, a book intended largely for the student who is interested in the entire field of modern drama, containing a large number of reading references.

"The Theory and Technique of Playwriting" by JOHN HOWARD LAWSON, the latest and one of the best books for the practising playwright.

"Our Theatre Today" edited by HERSCHEL L. BRICKER, a composite text-book by thirteen theatre experts on the art and craft of the modern theatre.

SDC Staff

Laura Penn	Executive Director
Mauro Melleno	Director of Contracts
Sam Bellinger	Director of Finance and Membership
Karina Miller	Director of 50th Anniversary Initiative
Barbara Wolkoff	Senior Contract Administrator
Randy Anderson	Contract Administrator
Renee Lasher	Contract Administrator
Evan Shoemake	Contract Administrator
Gretchen Michelfeld	Membership Coordinator
Michele Holmes	Senior Business Associate
Kim Rogers	Business Associate
Preston Copley	Executive Assistant
Lena Abrams	Administrative Assistant

SDC Mission

To foster a national community of professional stage Directors and Choreographers by protecting the rights, health and livelihoods of all our members. To facilitate the exchange of ideas, information and opportunities, while educating the current and future generations about the role of Directors and Choreographers and providing effective administration, negotiations and contractual support.

www.ingramcontent.com/pod-product-compliance
Lightning Source LLC
Chambersburg PA
CBHW062153080426
42734CB00010B/1668